Christine and Graham Shaw have lived in Dorset for eight years, during which time they have visited every garden in the county that opens to the public, many two or even three times. For *The Dorset Garden Guide* all the gardens had to be visited again, so that Christine could make notes for her text and Graham take the superb colour photographs that illustrate the book.

Christine has written articles for many national gardening magazines, and enjoys bold planting schemes and a clever use of colour. Since working on the book, she has grown increasingly fond of old roses and the quieter herbaceous perennials. Graham trained as an architect, and is interested in the relationship between house and garden.

Their other interests include music, the theatre, walking, and long lazy holidays in France. The summers however are reserved for Dorset and their own garden at the aptly-named Rose Cottage — which they both admit still has a long way to go!

GW00597358

FRONTISPIECE *The gardens at the Manor House, Hinton St Mary.*

The Dorset Garden Guide

Christine and Graham Shaw

Dovecote Press

For Nan and her love of gardening –
for Grandad who, uncomplainingly, did so much of the work.

First published in 1991 by the Dovecote Press Ltd
Stanbridge, Wimborne, Dorset BH21 4JD
ISBN 0 946159 87 4

© Christine and Graham Shaw 1991

Designed by Humphrey Stone
Photoset by The Typesetting Bureau Ltd, Wimborne, Dorset
Origination by Chroma Graphics (Overseas) Pte Ltd, Singapore
Printed by Kim Hup Lee Printing Co Pte Ltd, Singapore

Contents

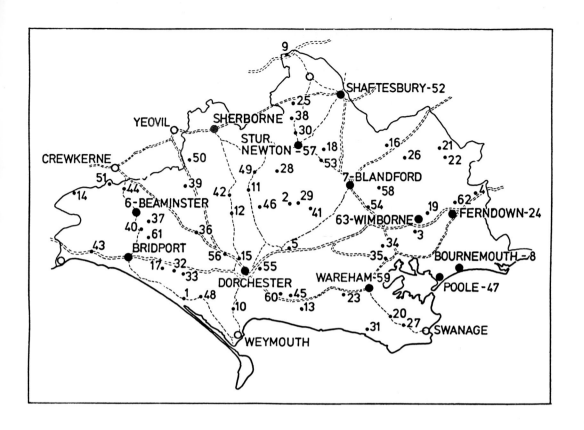

Introduction

Collecting together in book form gardens of Dorset that are open to the public has been an idea of mine for some time. It reached fruition when I found that David Burnett at the Dovecote Press had also been mulling over the possibilities, but was waiting for a time when he could produce a book in full colour. The time, he felt, had arrived; the seed had germinated.

Armed with the 'yellow book' of the National Gardens Scheme for initial guidance I planned my way around dozens of gardens over the spring and summer months. The National Gardens Scheme Charitable Trust was the forerunner of 'gardens open'. To these I added gardens that open for other charities – notably the Red Cross – and the villages that offer a fund-raising Garden Walkabout. Cerne Abbas is an old hand here, the garden weekend having taken place in June for the last 15 years; there are many others. Trying to fit every garden in at its best opening time, my visiting schedule was like a giant jig-saw puzzle. I wrestled with the problem of whether or not to be selective, as just talking to fellow garden visitors soon made me realise that there were gardens high on any list, and those not quite so remarkable.

Early visits soon proved, though, that every garden has something to offer. Ranging from grand and formal Italianate-style, through natural woodland to manicured suburbia, each one has an idea for the keen gardener to 'steal': an unusual colour combination, a new plant, a clever use of space. Armchair gardeners will find many places in which it is pleasant just to sit and enjoy the surroundings.

This is not intended to be a gardening book, so much as a book for the enjoyment of gardens. I have used both common and Latin names. Where plants could be specifically identified, I have done so; otherwise I have referred to them in general terms.

Garden owners contributed enormously to my enjoyment as well as to my knowledge. Most had a tale to tell. My favourite is from a garden that is an imaginative green haven of mainly foliage plants, some common, many rare. It was visited by a sturdy northener, shirt-sleeves and braces, who dashed round the paths and headed for the exit gate in less than five minutes. As he caught the astonished look on the owner's face, he said: "Eeh! All you've got's a few Busy Lizzies!"

If nothing else, it proved a point. Different people look for different things in a garden. Those gardens that I have visited, between them, have something for everyone. It is up to you to find your favourite, and I know you will enjoy the search.

Acknowledgements

I would like to thank all garden owners who spared time to show me round, pointed out their successes, and invited me to commiserate in their disappointments. 1990 began with 'the storm', and many gardens suffered terrible wind damage. Owners barely had time to draw breath before Dorset was hit by some of the hardest, latest frosts on record; but gardeners never give up. Even while clearance work was in progress and frost-dead plants being reduced to compost, they were planning for the future. Long may they continue!

"The answer", as all good gardeners know, "lies in the soil". The geology of Dorset is complicated, and varied. My thanks to Geoffrey Poole MA, for clarifying the geological strata and it's relevance to gardening in the county.

I am indebted to the following owners who have given permission for their own colour slides to be reproduced: Mrs Beryl Askew (Dymond's Folly); David Dampney (Boveridge Farm); Alan Stevens (Ivy Cottage, cover); Sir Robert Williams (Little Platt). I am also grateful to George Wright for the photograph of Cranborne Manor gardens.

Thanks, also, to Derek Beauchamp and John Christmas, who on first hearing of the project insisted I made use of their office word processor. It has made life so much easier – and quicker – and is a facility I have much appreciated.

Finally, so much is due to Graham who covered the miles with me from start to finish. He has provided encouragement as well as the photographs and drawings, and philosophically accepted the hectic schedule I imposed. It has been a marvellous summer.

CHRISTINE SHAW
Charminster

9

Opening Arrangements and Information

Opening times of the smaller private gardens do alter from year to year.

If a garden is open under the National Gardens Scheme it will be listed in the 'yellow book' that is published annually. It is important to obtain an up-to-date copy of the booklet. Gardeners opt in and out of the Scheme, so always double check. The Dorset brochure is available free in libraries and some bookshops, and gives names of County Organisers who are happy to provide additional information.

Funds raised under the Scheme go to the Queen's Nursing Institute to help district nurses and other nurses in need. While this original cause still benefits, so do additional charities as the amount of money raised each year – around 1 million – steadily increases. Gardens open for other charities are usually advertised in the local press. The *Western Gazette* has a 'Gardens Open' section every week, covering not just Dorset but also neighbouring counties. The *Dorset Evening Echo* gives some coverage, depending on space, and the free *Blackmore Vale Magazine* prints local details each week.

Where a garden is open 'by appointment', a telephone number is given on the appropriate page and the owner will be pleased to hear from you to arrange a date and time. Do take advantage of this. You really will be welcome! Owners are happy to let you browse, or to be on hand if there are questions you would like to ask.

Don't ignore the garden walkabouts: when individual villages open many of their gardens. They all advertise: in the local press, libraries, posters, handouts, parish magazines. For a very modest cost, or a donation, a wide selection of gardens can be enjoyed, usually on a Sunday afternoon. Teas are provided by many, from a welcome cup to a full Dorset cream tea, and there are occasionally plants for sale.

Do, please, respect the privacy of owners on days when they are not advertised as being open. Even if you are passing the door, resist the temptation – you might be the twentieth 'just passing' that week. You will be very welcome at advertised times. With very few exceptions, only guide dogs are admitted to gardens. If you are unsure whether you will be able to park your car in a shady position, it is preferable to leave your pet at home; you can then both enjoy the garden visit.

Other organisations I came into contact with on my visits included the Dorset Gardens Trust. It's aims are: "To preserve, enhance and re-create for the enjoyment and education of the public whatever garden land may exist or has existed within the County of Dorset." The Trust is funded through membership subscriptions, donations, grants and fund-raising activities, and is always looking for volunteers to help in their important work. Further details are available from Dorset County Council, County Hall, Dorchester.

The National Council for the Conservation of Plants and Gardens is also supported by many garden owners, and is one of the reasons why there are so many unusual plants to be seen on your visits. There are over 1000 different cultivated plants lost each year. These plants are destroyed by disease, fail because they are difficult to propagate, or just "go out of fashion" and eventually disappear. The NCCPG is working to conserve endangered plants. For details of your own County Group, contact the NCCPG, c/o RHS Wisley Gardens, Woking, Surrey, GU23 6QB.

A garden figure at Forde Abbey.

Abbotsbury

Sub-tropical Gardens

B3157 Weymouth/
Bridport, just west of
Abbotsbury village.

Open daily spring to
autumn. Tel: 0305-871387
for information. Wheelchair
access. Plant sales. Teas.

*Sub-tropical Gardens. Lush
foliage in the river valley at
Abbotsbury.*

Abbotsbury Sub-tropical Gardens occupy 20 acres of valley land, tucked in between the folded hillsides of the Dorset coast. The high canopy of trees and mild climate make Abbotsbury a colourful place to visit before other less sheltered gardens have started their season. The original gardens of 1760 were considerably extended in the 19th century, and expansion is still taking place.

Although Abbotsbury gardens make an interesting and enjoyable visit at any time, they are essentially a place to enjoy spring and early summer colour. The walled garden of camellias is a heady delight, with pink, red and white flowers among the glossy dark green foliage. Azaleas and rhododendrons create banks of colour under the tree canopy, with a wide variety of more tender trees and shrubs. In summer, the roses come into their own. Tree paeonies and other flowering shrubs fill the gardens in a profusion of colour. Narrow paths criss-cross the valley, with the stream in the bottom edged by moisture loving plants and spanned by small bridges.

By August the hydrangea walk is beautiful, with pink, blue, and every combination of the two delicately tinting the lacecaps and mop heads. Abbotsbury has lily ponds, a conservatory, bamboo ride and peat garden, among other features. There is also a shop and garden centre, and a small tea garden. Peacocks strut among the borders.

The gardens are inevitably linked with the Swannery, and a combined admission ticket can be bought at either. Chesil Beach can be easily reached on the narrow road that passes the gardens. Abbotsbury village, which dates from medieval times, provides an ideal place to pause and enjoy this part of Dorset's coast.

Ansty

Aller Green
Aller Lane

Approaching Ansty from
the Cheselbourne road, turn
right just before the Fox Inn
into Aller Lane. Aller Green
is first on left.

Open for NGS, and other
charities. Teas at Ivy
Cottage, Aller Lane, open at
same time. Combined
admission.

The old thatched cottage firmly in command of its plot sets the scene for this garden. It is an old fashioned cottage garden of approximately one acre that has survived the passage of time. Mr A. Thomas has lived at Aller Green man and boy, as did his father and grandfather before him.

The trees and shrubs have matured into a wonderfully informal setting, with new varieties being introduced to replace the older wood. Sadly, an ancient walnut tree was lost to the 89/90 gales; another fallen tree, now sturdily propped, supports *Rosa multiflora* 'Grevillei' – the Seven Sisters Rose.

The garden wanders, in higgledy-piggledy fashion, up to a triangular vegetable plot. The vegetables are planted in well- ordered rows, but are charmingly jostled for space by large clumps of herbaceous perennials and spring flowering bulbs. The surrounding hedgerows surprise, with *Amelanchier canadensis*, *Ribes sanguineum* and *Exochorda x macrantha* tucked in amongst the green.

Tulips spill out of varied containers, providing bright splashes of

13

Dorset cottage garden at Aller Green.

colour against the more refined fritillaries. A small garden store is almost completely covered with ivy. Mr Thomas says he has no overall plan – everything just gets put in where there is room. The result is a charming cottage garden, in the true meaning of the words.

Ansty

Ivy Cottage
Aller Lane

Approaching Ansty from the Cheselbourne road, turn right just before the Fox Inn into Aller Lane. Ivy Cottage is about 500 yards on left.

This is a garden that you see from the road as you approach, glimpse across the hedge as you park, and can't wait to get inside. Ivy Cottage has been the lovely thatched home of Anne and Alan Stevens since 1963. During that time a garden has been reclaimed from what was a wilderness of weeds, nettles and withy beds.

Nestling deep in a hollow, the garden is crossed by a stream; spring water also creates permanently boggy areas away from the main stream. With chalk fields on one side, the garden slopes down to a more acid soil. It forms a pocket for late frosts. The whole combines to give diverse gardening conditions, of which the Stevens' have made perfect use. It is obvious from talking to fellow visitors that this is one of Dorset's most highly-regarded gardens.

A raised border close to the cottage gives the driest conditions. This is

Open some Sun afternoons for NGS, and other charities. Also every Thur April/mid October, 10 – 5 pm. Tel: Milton Abbas 880053 for group visits. Plant sales. Teas.

For illustration see front cover.

ideal for penstemmons, salvias, pulsatillas and a wide collection of alliums. It is a good vantage point to enjoy the wide, curving herbaceous borders as far as the beautiful blue *Cedrus atlantica glauca.* Hundreds of perennials provide an eye-catching display from spring through to autumn.

Good foliage plants include *Hosta fortunei* 'Halcyon' and 'Albopicta'; *Ajuga reptans* 'Rainbow'; *Euphorbia polychroma* plus golden thyme. *Hemerocallis* (day lilies) include the lovely 'Kwanso Variegata' form, with delphiniums and *Aruncus dioicus* for added height. Trollius and lobelia fill in between – National Collections of both are held at Ivy Cottage.

There are many mature trees forming a high canopy, including *Davidia involucrata*, the handkerchief tree. The acid soil is suitable for azaleas and camellias, which give early spring colour.

The vegetable and fruit garden is tucked away behind a neat hedge of *Lonicera nitida.* Even here the beds are decorative, edged with parsley and the red leaf lettuce.

The stream winds its way between large patches of golden marsh marigolds, and the wet conditions suit many varieties of primula. Giant *Gunnera manicata* provides statuesque height, its stems reaching 7 feet under ideal conditions, and the acid yellow *Lysichiton americanus* is an unusual addition.

There is another small stream bordering the garden, banked with primroses, bluebells, honesty and many ferns. Not a yard of space is wasted or untended. Raised alpine beds and sink gardens next to the cottage contain the smaller plants.

Ashington

Heatherwood Nurseries

A349 Wimborne/Poole. Turn right to Ashington about 1 mile south of Wimborne. Garden approximately 3/4 mile on left.

Open every day from 9 – 5, Sun 9 – 12, with the exception of the Christmas/ New Year period.

Mr and Mrs Ronald Squires have been gardening for many years, a small nursery in Ashington village expanding to the present site. They specialise in heathers, and their own half acre garden next to the nursery is a superb example of heather gardening at its best.

The garden was originally rough heath land, and considerable clearance had to be carried out before lorry loads of top soil could be brought in to improve the site.

The wide borders were originally herbaceous but, when Mr Squires retired, he decided on easy maintenance. The garden now has wide drifts of heathers, about 800 in fifty different varieties, with colour of either foliage or flower the whole year round.

The borders have been sloped slightly up and away from the lawn, so that the garden room and windows of the house have the fullest possible views. Several hundred small conifers break up the heather beds, with acers and azaleas adding spring and autumn colour.

A recent addition has been a small pool and rockery, where the garden is entered through a rustic arch.

Many plants featured in the garden are available in the adjacent nursery, while the Squires' will provide all the ideas you could need for a successful, colourful, year-round display.

The Glade – tailored green and cream.

Ashley Heath

37 The Glade

A31 Wimborne/
Ringwood, Ashley Heath
roundabout. Turn north
west to Ashley Heath. Left
into Lions Lane just before
the 'Forge' PO. The Glade is
first left, with No 37 on
right.

Open for NGS.

Nearly at the end of the gardening season I called on Mrs Sally Tidd at 37 The Glade. It was a long, sunny drive, but worth every hot mile, and this is high on my list of gardens not to be missed.

The garden is fairly small, but by cleverly disguising the boundaries it appears to stretch much further. A shady glade of trees links it to adjacent land.

I thoroughly enjoyed the collection of variegated plants and shrubs; so many in one garden, to stunning effect. From tiny ground cover plants to mature acers and cornus, the creams and golds of the different foliages lighten the whole garden. Indeed, this is very much a garden where the background foliage sets the scene. Contrast has also been achieved with leaf shape; spiky foliage against large leaves, feathery fronds against solid.

One side border swings diagonally across the lawn, almost bisecting the garden, giving the opportunity to meander further and discover hidden treasures. A paved circle with fountain creates a focal point.

This is poor soil, heath sand over clay. Mr and Mrs Tidd have been here since 1974, from the 'building site' stage. Everything possible has been added to the soil in an attempt to keep it workable, including coarse sand, mushroom compost, and horse manure. The results are worthwhile.

Especially of note were 'Flamingo', a variegated cream and green acer with pink tips, the huge greeny-white heads of *Hydrangea arborescens* 'Grandiflora', and the tall mauve stems of *Verbena bonariensis* which give clouds of colour without obstructing the view.

Athelhampton

Athelhampton House

A35 east of Puddletown, on
north of road.

Open Wed, Thur, Sun and
Bank Hols from the Wed
before Easter until
November. Also Mon and
Tue in August. 2 – 6 pm.
Wheelchair access. Teas.
Enquiries tel: 0305-848363.

Athelhampton House was built by Sir William Martyn in "about the year of the Battle of Bosworth Field". Sir William, who was to become a Mayor of London, was given a licence to build a house with battlements and towers, and to enclose 160 acres of deer park. Over the ensuing centuries the house passed through several families. The formal gardens were designed by Francis Inigo Thomas, and are still laid out in a series of walled courts.

Attractive thatched outbuildings form the entrance, from where a grass walk between clipped yew hedges leads to the River Piddle. Broad sweeping lawns separate house from river on the north, and there are seats facing lovely views to the countryside beyond.

Athelhampton has many small gardens, a progression of spaces through decorative gates and high walls. Water features widely, with lily ponds and fountains, subtle trickles and more exuberant cascades.

The Great Court with its triangular clipped yews is overlooked by the Terrace, which has a small pavilion either end – one for Joy and Summer, the other for Sorrow and Winter. The Corona has walls of curves and

OPPOSITE *Each gateway at Athelhampton reveals yet another aspect of the gardens.*

obelisks in an Elizabethan style. The curved ends of the rectangular pond in the Private Garden echo the shape of the Great Hall roof.

Athelhampton gardens have received many gifts, including a collection of rock-plants from the Abbey Gardens at Tresco. These, with other plants preferring a dry position, are housed in the Lion's Mouth! There is a fine walled kitchen garden of one acre. A central pond is reached through an apple and laburnum walk, and British varieties of apples are planted around the perimeter.

The gardens are continually being enlarged, and a haven for wildlife has recently been created on seven acres to the north and west. Athelhampton's gardens are amongst the most interesting in the county, and enjoy a glorious setting.

Beaminster

Parnham House

A3066 Beaminster/ Bridport. Parnham is on right heading south, just outside Beaminster.

Open from 1 April/end October, 10 – 5pm, Wed, Sun, Bank Hols. Groups by prior appointment Tue and Thur, tel: Beaminster 862204. Wheelchair access. Light lunches and teas.

Mellow brick paving complements the warm colours of Parnham's herbaceous border.

Parnham, the home of Mr and Mrs John Makepeace, sits squarely in the middle of a wooded valley. The grounds are encompassed by walls and low stone edgings, inside which the formal gardens are beautifully maintained. Beyond the boundaries, the trees clothe the valley sides.

It is interesting to compare this garden with that of Mapperton "just up the road", where the garden, also in a valley, fades quietly into open countryside. At Parnham the gardens have been shaped and pruned, but sharply delineated from the countryside, providing a formal and totally appropriate setting for the house.

Parnham dates from 1540, but was substantially reconstructed early

this century. The car park adjoins the river, and there are pretty walks along the banks as well as a picnic area.

The house stands well above the river, and the main formal gardens are to the south. The wide Ladies' Terrace with its balustrades and gazebos provides a view down to the Yew Terrace, with fifty clipped yews impressive in their uniformity.

Water pours down both terraces — no informal tumbling, but canalised beside the steps, disappearing eventually towards the recently restored lake.

The East Court is now surrounded by climbing roses, both on the old stone walls and scrambling up free-standing classic columns.

To the north are the herbaceous borders, backed by a high brick wall with an attractive herringbone brick path for access. One border glows with yellow, orange and red; the other is planted in soft blue, mauve and pink.

Parnham House is also partially open, and rooms on view include the John Makepeace Furniture Workshops.

Blandford Forum

Stour House
East Street

Off the one-way system in central Blandford, just before reaching the market place, on left.

Open for NGS. Wheelchair access to main garden. Plant sales. Teas.

Stour House is a Georgian town house, with gardens of 2.5 acres extending to an island in the River Stour. The amazing thing about this garden in the centre of Blandford is that it exists at all. The lovely house fronts Blandford's busy road system, giving no hint of the extensive gardens beyond.

The garden is walled, the mellow red brick boundaries supporting many shrubs and climbers, including the early clematis varieties. The main south garden has wide herbaceous borders and a small pond, which extend the interest well into the summer.

The lawns reach towards the River Stour, and in spring a swathe cut through the long grass of the orchard leads through a carpet of daffodils to an amazing bridge. Designed and constructed in 1987, it is made of iroko wood, and oak from Longleat.

The present owner, Mr T. Card, has been at Stour House since 1981. He has made many changes, and is now directing his energies to improve and plant the island in the Stour. This is a major part of the garden, and runs along the centre of the river behind many other houses, culminating in an impressive view of the weir. There are many mature trees underplanted with spring bulbs, and the whole forms a delightful walk in an otherwise unseen part of the town.

Bournemouth

Rosedene
98 Hill View Road
Ensbury Park

A347 Wimborne Road out of Bournemouth. After the roundabout at the junction with the A3060 (Castle Lane), turn left into Redhill Avenue and immediately right to Redhill Drive. Hillview Road is second on right.

Open for NGS

When many gardens are past their best at the end of August, Rosedene is still full of interest. Mr and Mrs J. Hodges share an interest in fruit, and this small but productive garden has many varieties.

The garden has been designed firstly to allow the owners to expand their interest in fruit, particularly grapes, but also to be a garden that can still be managed and enjoyed in retirement.

The front garden is paved except for a large raised central bed, which when I visited was massed with 'Bizzie Lizzies' all grown from seed.

About one third of the back garden is covered by a pergola, and is again paved around a large pond and rockery. *Clematis armandii*, wisteria and other climbers overhang. The garden walls are high, supporting twenty four espalier fruit trees – damson, plum, apples, cherry and a thornless blackberry among others.

An unusual solar dome contains four varieties of grape: 'Royal Muscadine', 'Riesling Sylvaner', 'Muller Thugau', and the Strawberry Grape. These are all dessert fruit, grown without any winter heat and free of chemical sprays.

A narrow greenhouse at the end of the garden has more grapes, including 'Black Hamburgh', also peach, nectarine, kiwi fruit and cucumber plants, together with jasmine. Outside are gooseberries and blackcurrants.

The garden was started in 1980 and took about 10 years to reach maturity. It gives an interesting insight into gardening on a small scale, especially in a town environment.

Bournemouth

46 Roslin Road South
Talbot Woods

A3049 into Bournemouth past Wallisdown to Talbot Roundabout. Right into Glenferness Avenue, first right into Roslin Road South. No 46 is on right.

Open for NGS, also by appointment tel: 0202 – 510243. Plant sales.

This garden has been cleverly divided to form several smaller areas. Immediately behind the house a small lawn, pond and paved area for sitting out are surrounded by raised beds full of colour. Small shrubs and perennials are combined in a scheme that is full but not fussy, chosen to provide interest twelve months of the year, and which also demonstrates excellent use of a comparatively small town garden.

A pergola of climbing roses and clematis links this with a second paved space, more secluded, also with a small pond. Plant containers and old chimney pots of pelargoniums add to the colourful borders. The vegetable garden, greenhouse and soft fruit bushes are at the far end, and room has been found for a cold frame and compost bins.

Continuing round the garden a path leads back to the house, past a neat rockery with rock roses, osteospermums, diascia, and then on to side and front gardens which are similarly colourful.

Bournemouth

Waterfalls
59 Branksome Wood Road

Take the main road out of Bournemouth centre that runs on the right side of the Upper Central Gardens. Waterfalls is on the right.

Open for NGS.

TOP *Stunning Waterfalls near Bournemouth's busy centre.*

BOTTOM *The woodland walk provides a complete contrast to the colourful garden at Chiffchaffs.*

Mr and Mrs Roger Butler, faced with what for many could prove to be an impossible site, accepted the problems head on. A narrow plot, extending upwards at a very steep angle, cries out for a mini waterfall.

The garden is so enclosed by tall trees that it resembles a green cavern. A small and immaculate lawn surrounds a pond. The water tumbles in a series of small cascades down terraces of greenery: laurel, ferns, hostas, a statuesque castor oil plant, The sunlight picks out the few patches of colour provided by a pot of geraniums, a fuchsia, a deep red paeony and mauve foxgloves. Reflected in the pond are two or three huge clumps of white arum lily.

Climb the steep steps up the terracing, through an arch heavy with honeysuckle and clematis, and reach the small plateau at the 'top' of the garden. The loss of several large trees has opened this up the sky, and now mahonias and acers have a chance to thrive. You will also find the source of the waterfall. The view from the top includes a pretty blue cedar and the soft green of larch. Steps down again are steep.

Visitors will remember the garden for a long time. it is small, elegant, unexpected and very different. Although the terracing is steep, the series of cascades are both imaginative and a delight.

Bourton

Chiffchaffs, Chaffeymoor

A303 at west end of Bourton, lane signed Chaffeymoor on right, heading west. Chiffchaffs is at top of lane, on right.

Garden open every Sun and Bank Hol Mon (2 – 5.30 pm) from April to September, except first Sun in the month. Also open last Wed in each month over the same period. Parties by appointment at other times, tel: Bourton 840841. Adjacent Abbey Plants nursery open Wed to Sat, 10 – 1, 2 – 5 pm. Also Sun afternoons when the garden is open. Teas on 2nd and 4th Sun, for NGS.

Mr and Mrs K. Potts first saw Chiffchaffs in the late 70s, when it was tumble-down and rat infested with 11 acres of overgrown land. Since buying it, the house has been beautifully restored and a garden planted; a small nursery adjacent does a thriving business in plants; distant woodland has become a blaze of colour with azaleas and rhododendrons where a woodland walk is being created.

The house is very much part of the garden. Plants grow up to it and over it in profusion, multi-layered in terraces that give far-reaching views to the south west. The beautiful pink *Rosa* 'Madame Grégoire Staechelin' climbs alongside red *R.* Étoile d'Hollande', with *Clematis* 'Mrs Cholmondeley', *C.* 'The President' and *C.* 'Nelly Moser'.

The garden is approached through an avenue of *Prunus sargentii* underplanted with daffodils. A small wicket gate takes you in past *Daphne burkwoodii* 'Somerset' with its heady perfume, the cream and yellow shrub rose 'Nevada', and *R.* 'Cramoise Superieure'. Crazy-paving leads alongside a small pond, the edges softened with bright rock roses. The large, daisly-like heads of osteospermums form cool drifts of white, through pale pink to soft mauve.

Acers, azaleas and rhododendrons are a blaze of early colour, with foliage interest including the *Berberis thunbergii* 'Aurea', *Rhus Cotinus*, and many varieties of hostas.

At the top of the terracing a hedge hides the vegetable patch; a sheltered site for a seat gives lovely views through carefully planned

23

"windows" in the surrounding shrubs. *Abutilon* 'Tennant's White' was in magnificent bloom early in the year.

The woodland walk, a gentle stroll away, is a contrast. The way lies under mature trees, where the ground is carpeted with bluebells. Underground springs create perfect boggy conditions for the plum coloured *Primula pulverulenta.* This used to be an alder wood, and some of the trees have been kept to maintain the light woodland conditions that are so ideal.

Bourton

Snape Cottage
Chaffeymoor

A303, west end of Bourton, lane signed to Chaffeymoor on right heading west. Snape Cottage at top end of lane, on left.

Snape Cottage opens mid April to early July in conjunction with Chiffchaffs for NGS, and they are two gardens worth travelling to see. Plant sales.

Mr and Mrs I. Whinfield arrived at Snape Cottage in 1988, with a separate lorry for more than 400 plants they had begged from friends and neighbours to begin their garden. They have been collecting ever since, and the garden is taking shape with an amazing variety of the less common plants. Most are labelled.

Angela Whinfield, a self-confessed devotee of Margery Fish, is a most knowledgeable plantswoman. Her particular interests are the 16th and 17th century varieties of pinks and wallflowers, and she has a wide selection of auriculas. Her aim is to put each plant in the ideal situation, not just planning the overall effect. If a plant is unhappy, she moves it promptly.

Ian Whinfield has used his landscaping skills to good effect on this gently sloping site. The couple are conservation conscious, growing comfrey for use as a high nitrogen fertiliser on the garden, and setting aside a small area for a wild garden.

The garden is sheltered by stone walls and beech hedges, but views to the south west stretch into the distance, to Bulbarrow on a clear day.

Full perennial borders include variegated foliage plants such as *Ruta graveolens*, and *Veronica gentianoides*. Hardy geraniums, too: *Geranium madarense*, with its deep magenta flowers; *G. renardii*, pale lavender, purple veined; *G. dalmaticum*, light pink, with foliage that colours well in autumn. There are many others.

An herbaceous border has also been cut across the sweep of the garden, linked to the upper terrace by a trellis with climbing roses and the greeny-white *Clematis* 'Duchess of Edinburgh'. This is a cottage garden border, with tall delphiniums, paeonies, erigerons, iris, phlox and hostas. This section of the garden has underground springs, and moisture loving plants such as *Gunnera manicata* are the basis for a new bed.

Broadwey

Higher Manor Farm

A354 Dorchester/
Weymouth. Swan Inn is on
right heading south. Turn
right just before inn into
Littlemead, and the farm is
at the end of the lane.

Open for NGS. Plant sales.
Teas at Upwey Wishing
Well

An aerial photograph of the farm in the drought of 1976 shows a small bungalow surrounded by a brown wasteland, the whole overlooked by a line of unremarkable Scots pines. Since then Sarah Studley, who works full-time on her husband's dairy farm, has worked miracles.

Higher Manor Farm now boasts a lush garden under mature trees, with many unusual plants. It is a secret garden, with narrow twisting paths linking from one section to the next. It is difficult to see soil anywhere – Sarah is a self-confessed "poker-inner"! The result is a garden that is full of interest, in colour and in form. There are no far vistas; rather a well controlled riot of plants everywhere.

A weird and wonderful *Aeonium arboreum* provides a central feature in a black/burgundy border. This succulent has fleshy rosettes of shiny dark burgundy. It settles quite happily in the border each summer, but needs greenhouse protection to over- winter. The nearby perennial astilea is aptly named 'Silver Sword'. Old favourites blend with the more unusual plants. One you definitely won't see anywhere else is a variegated hosta called 'Sarah Studley', a sport that its namesake has grown on with much excitement. Interesting variegated foliage plants, always a favourite of mine, include *Phlox paniculata* 'Nora Leigh' and *Salix integra* 'Hakuro Nikishi', here allowed to reach medium shrub size.

A fairly new addition is a pergola, almost hidden between two shrubby parts of the garden which it now neatly links. Stone steps rise beneath climbing *Rosa* 'Cécile Brunner', *Clematis* 'Marie Boisselot', *C.* 'Elsa Spath' and *C.* 'Henryi'. A waterfall is planned for the large formal pond, towered over by the 6' flower spires of yellow *Iris pseudacorus*.

Visitors to the garden are often as interested in the birds and animals nearby. Colourful macaws gave a noisy commentary as we passed and, out through the farm, two Chinese geese were casting covetous eyes at anything edible.

Buckland Newton

Dominey's Yard

B3143 Piddle Valley road to
village. 'No through road'
between Gaggle of Geese
pub, and church. House on
left.

Open for NGS, also by
appointment tel:
030-05-295. Teas.

The gardens surrounding this 17th century thatched cottage were begun by Mr and Mrs W. Gueterbock in 1965. Mature trees and shrubs screen the garden and divide it into several contrasting areas.

The far end of the garden is on greensand. This acid soil is ideal for camellias, and there are many different varieties to provide spring colour, together with magnolias, and bulbs.

Nearer the house the soil becomes limey, and roses (including many varieties of old fashioned and Himalayan climbing roses), plus flowering shrubs, clematis and lilies extend the flowering season into the summer.

Autumn colour is provided by cyclamen, acers, azaleas and spindles amongst others. The winter sees berries, coloured stems and unusual bark maintaining the interest. At the front of the house, tubs of variegated foliage and lilies contrast well with the darker greens by the house wall.

There are several lovely specimen trees, including *Acer griseum* with its attractive peeling bark. It provides spectacular autumn colour. There are splendid views across open countryside beyond the garden. The garden is at about 500 feet above sea level and this, combined with shelter from the west, provides a micro- climate which favours less hardy plants. This has helped the owners fashion a garden for all seasons.

Dominey's Yard, the house providing the perfect backdrop.

Hundreds of herbaceous plants await discovery in Sticky Wicket's unconventional Round Garden.

Buckland Newton

Sticky Wicket

B3143 Piddle Valley road to village. Sticky Wicket is on right beyond church.

Open for NGS, also every Thur mid May/Sept, 10 – 6.30 pm. Parties by appointment, tel: 030-05-476. Wheelchair access (gravel paths). Plant sales. Teas.

Peter and Pam Lewis have conjured a garden out of nothing, and the end result is totally different from anything I have seen before. Since 1986 they have transformed nearly 4 acres of pasture into the Lower Gardens, and the unconventional Round Garden.

The Lewis's are conscious of the need to create and maintain an ecologically balanced garden, which complements and forms part of the surrounding countryside. Butterfly and insect attracting plants feature widely, plus many herbs. There is also a small pond which is home to frogs and dragonflies, as well as flowers.

The Lower Gardens surround the house, and clever colour grouping of shrubs and perennials provides visual appeal whichever way you look. Several small pergolas act as links between house and garden, a small conservatory serving the same purpose to the south.

In the Round Garden, gravel paths have been laid in concentric circles

27

like ripples in a pond. Straight paths from centre to edge divide the circles into segments. The resulting arc-shaped beds are tightly planted with cottage garden plants, herbs and shrubs. In August the overlying theme appeared to be blues and mauves, with lavender and catmint spilling over onto the paths.

The Round Garden is an excellent place to explore, to decide what to plant, and what groups of plants look good together. This is exactly the way Pam uses it. These beds are where she satisfies herself that a scheme will work, before transferring the idea to one of the many private gardens she has helped design and maintain.

Sticky Wicket has more than 500 varieties of herbaceous plants and 150 varieties of herbs. Foliage plants, especially evergreen and grey, provide interest throughout the year.

In 1990 a white woodland garden was in its infancy, extending cultivation further away from the house. A wild garden is planned for the future.

Pam and Peter provide plenty of information about their garden on your visit, and describe it as 'a romantic garden designed more for the artist and naturalist than for those seeking botanical or horticultural excellence'.

Cerne Abbas

Village gardens

A352 Dorchester/
Sherborne, 6 miles north of
Dorchester.

About thirty gardens at Cerne Abbas open their gates to the public each summer to raise money for charity. The venture began in 1975 when the Parochial Church Council put forward the scheme to raise money for bells in the village church. The Open Weekend was so popular it became an annual event, and the scheme has raised more than £13,500 since it's beginning.

The gardens are always open the third weekend in June, from 2 – 6 pm both days. A daily one price ticket provides entry. The event is widely publicised in the press, and through leaflets available at local libraries and Tourist Information centres. There is ample parking in Simsay, at the western end of the village, which is well signed and marshalled.

More than 2,000 visitors each year take advantage of the Open Weekend to enjoy a village that is one of Dorset's major tourist attractions. The gardens are mostly small scale, ranging from old fashioned cottage to immaculate modern. Several have the River Cerne running through them.

Teas are provided by the local WI. There is also a plant sale in the centre of the village, a crèche, and a cool place to leave your plant purchases until you are ready to leave. Only the stout-hearted should consider seeing all the gardens in one afternoon; much better to take a picnic, explore the Cerne Giant, and enjoy a leisurely selection.

Striking colours in one of Cerne's open gardens.

Chaldon Herring

The Manor House

A352 Dorchester/ Wareham. Turn south to East Chaldon, bear right in village. Manor House is adjacent to church, on left.

Open for NGS and is, I think, the only garden in Dorset to open from 4 – 8 pm. This is a time of day when the softer light is kind to plants, and when elderly people in particular might prefer to venture out in the cool of the day. Also open occasionally for other charities. Plant sales. Teas.

If you love herbaceous borders, then don't miss the chance to visit Dale and Alice Fishburn's 2 acre garden at Chaldon Herring. The Fishburns inherited a few flower beds and thirteen sculpted yew bushes. The un-lucky thirteenth was removed to make way for a decorative seat over-hung with creamy white *Rosa* 'Albéric Barbier', and the architectural yews are now symmetrical in the main large lawn. At the edge of the mown grass a wild area of steep bank drops to front garden level, with views over the hillsides beyond.

Brick pillars lead through to the kitchen garden where mellow brick paths divide the beds from a colourful flower border. There is a tiny 'stable garden' behind the old outbuildings. It is full of shrub roses, and the lovely green and white *Clematis* 'Alba luxurians'.

Tucked behind the main house is another small shed almost disappear-ing under *Clematis fargesii* – this is a great garden for climbers – then a stone flagged yard with an old pump, a corps de ballet of lilies in terracotta pots, followed by a vine hung pergola.

Yet another paved terrace leads to the main garden. Here the house wall is cascading with pink roses and blue clematis, which deserve atten-tion before the gaze becomes riveted on the huge herbaceous border.

29

The tops of two 'lobster pot' supports can just be seen, as this wonderful border reaches full height at the Manor House.

Alice Fishburn visited Sissinghurst, and saw there how herbaceous plants are supported by pea sticks woven into 'lobster pots'. It is an idea she has copied and, after much trial and error, has perfected her own way of weaving the supports. They are remarkably strong when finished and, in theory, should completely disappear as the border reaches its prime. It takes Alice about three weeks to weave the whole border, which is backed by pillar roses and clematis, with a raised grass path giving easy access behind the bed.

A wrought iron screen set in a formal arch at one end of the garden gives views through to the countryside, and a pergola on the end of the house is covered with climbers.

Alice remarked that she has given up much to provide the time to tend her garden, and was always reminded of a fellow gardener who said gardening was "eleven months hard labour, and one month acute disappointment"! I found no disappointments at the Manor House — only that I ran out of time.

Chard

Forde Abbey

Forde Abbey is in the south quadrant of the X roads formed by the B3167 and B3162, just south east of Chard. It is well signposted throughout the area.

Thirty acres of gardens surround this beautiful house, which was founded by Cistercian monks as a monastery more than 800 years ago. The best-known view of Forde Abbey is taken from west to east along the front of the house, with the long herbaceous border in the foreground.

This splendid border edges the Long Pond, and can be enjoyed either by walking along the adjacent pathway or by crossing to the other side of the water and looking back at the border and its reflections. Perennials can be enjoyed on a grand scale, and from mid summer onwards bright dahlias help to extend the display. It is worth noting the mechanics of

such a large border. Wide mesh green plastic net supported on short, stout posts provides a support at about 18″ high for the plants to grow through – much neater than individual staking, and very effective.

The Mermaid Pond is thickly carpeted with water-lilies, and there is a delightful small arbour on the bank. A short walk away is the Great Pond, with swans and moorhens paddling peacefully. This lake feeds the bog garden – one of the best I have seen. It is large enough to walk in and around, with several small streams.

Looking back to the house as you leave the Great Pond, there are wide views across the top and bottom lawns. Further afield, an avenue of limes frames the view as seen from the main entrance porch. There are many lovely trees, and mounded conifers and yews provide architectural features on the smooth lawns.

A Rock Garden leads to the Park Garden, and here again the clumps of perennials provide concentrated colour. Tall plumes of bocconia with attractive grey-green foliage look good at the back of the border; different shades of alstroemeria harmonise with white lilies; a scarlet climbing tropaeolum has almost covered its supporting shrub.

Make sure you leave time to admire the kitchen garden and to explore the excellent plant centre. The latter is only small, but has the more unusual plants for which a keen gardener might be searching.

Charminster

**Dymond's Folly
North Street**

A352 Dorchester/
Sherborne. North of
Charminster, right hand
side, just before
de-restriction sign.

Open privately once or
twice mid summer for local
charities, with local
advertising.

*Dymond's Folly, Eye-catching
colour early in the season.*

A walled garden leading down to the River Cerne, with mature shrubs and wide herbaceous borders, planted by John and Barbara Askew since 1965.

The garden immediately behind the house is protected by high walls, and herbaceous borders and shrubs have thrived. Tall evening primroses fill them with added colour late in the day.

A narrow break between shrubs leads through to the middle section of garden, where a greenhouse is enclosed by a wide curving herbaceous bed. Old apple trees support hanging baskets of pelargoniums, and more free-standing containers edge the borders. The curved border is well-planted and colourful, with groups of similar plants providing drifts of colour. Contrast is provided by the variegated sages, and silver foliaged artemisia.

At the bottom of the garden, a screen of shrubs and willows hides the river bank. A quiet seat under a laburnum tree looks the ideal place to spend a hot afternoon with a book.

Walking back to the house, *Clematis tangutica* is massed with yellow bells on the back wall. The door to the 'fernery' is open, and Barbara's collection of indoor plants is as interesting as those outside.

Chettle

Chettle House

A354 Blandford Forum/
Salisbury. Turn left to
Chettle heading north east.
View of house on left, pass
it, and swing left past
church.

Open daily except Tue, mid
April/October, 10 – 30 –
5.30 pm. Parties tel:
025-889209 for further
information. Wheelchair
access to gardens. Plant
sales. Teas.

ABOVE *Chettle's east front,
facing the formal gardens.*

No large formal gardens, no extensive parkland; instead, a very intimate setting for this 18th century gem. Thomas Archer was commissioned to build Chettle in 1710, to replace the Elizabethan home of the Chafin family. Although Chettle is now lived in as flats, Mr and Mrs Patrick Bourke open part of the lower house to the public.

The house is approached past the small garden centre and through a shrubbery. The view opens out, and two wide herbaceous borders joined by steps lead down to the west front and entry to the house.

On the south side, a vineyard faces the sun. This was started in 1981, the white table wines produced on the premises being for sale.

The main gardens are on the east front. A beautiful cedar occupies one corner of the lawns, and herbaceous and shrub borders provide a colourful edging. A stone balustraded terrace faces a long gravel walk, at the end of which the formal gardens merge easily into the surrounding farmland.

The domestic scale of Chettle is attractive, and house and gardens combined make a worthwhile visit.

Chilcombe

Chilcombe House

A35 Dorchester/Bridport.
Turn south off dual
carriageway, from either
direction. The lane into the
valley is narrow, with two
cattle grids; lovely views of
the sea as you descend.

Open for NGS. Plant sales.
Teas.

On a hillside facing south, this garden offers wide-ranging views of the countryside as well as the chance to enjoy a well-stocked and imaginative garden. It is a garden of lovely perfumes, contained by pergolas and enclosing hedges.

A small paved garden is planted in soft gentle colours, divided by low box hedges. A line of silver weeping pears overhangs. A very French courtyard at the entrance to the house has plants growing where they choose among the paving in informal fashion, and a small sign on the door, 'Chien Gentil'.

From the narrow lawn to the south, the ground drops away, balustraded by a lovely old stone wall, and the tops of roses beyond give a hint of the main garden. Above the roses the hills that edge the Dorset coast provide a superb view. The garden is fully planted with an abundance of perennials, roses, and clematis. Paths of grass, brick, or a combination of both make it easy to wander in this maze of colour. An idea worth remembering for even the smallest of gardens is the thyme bank, covered in white, pink and purple.

The vegetable garden is beautifully planted, everything spaced and bordered. The standard gooseberries are a marvellous idea – the fruit is at eye-level for picking. A small orchard off is the ideal place to rest on a hot summer's day, with the rose-covered walls providing shelter and privacy.

Chilcombe House is the home of John and Caryl Hubbard. John Hubbard's paintings are well known to many, and his artist's eye for colour is evident in the palette of the garden. The borders contain many unusual plants, and the plant sale that takes place on Chilcombe open days is a popular extra.

Chilcombe's paths, in a variety of textures, invite exploration.

34

Child Okeford

Russets
Rectory Lane

In village, take narrow road
by shops. Rectory Lane is
on right, and Russets is last
on right in lane.

Open for NGS, also by
appointment tel: Child
Okeford 860703.
Wheelchair access. Plant
sales. Teas.

ABOVE *Well-stocked borders at
Russets.*

A garden to be used and enjoyed, with paths between large irregular beds and plenty of sitting areas. It is a mature plot, started in 1972 from a neglected apple orchard. Of particular note is the eucalyptus in the front garden. The bark is mottled in wonderful colours, and the tree gives the lightest of shade.

There are plenty of large shrubs, including roses, many being used as support for clematis of which Mr and Mrs G. Harthan have nearly 40 varieties. Herbaceous perennials grow closely together, the newer pink/beige colours of achillea mingling with Michaelmas daisies at the end of the season. A sink garden holds a selection of alpines, with colourful plants in pots and tubs.

Gardens that encircle the house are always more interesting than plots you can take in at a glance, and this one is no exception. Grassy walks lead through the garden from fruit trees, to herbaceous, to shrubs, and to heathers. There is much to see, the peaceful location adding to the garden's charm.

Child Okeford

Wellington Lodge

From the centre of the village take the Shaftesbury road. The house is about 3/4 mile, on left.

Open for NGS. Teas. If there has been a rainy period, the owners recommend suitable footwear.

Mr and Mrs E. Graver bought Wellington Lodge in 1984. The gardens had already been laid out, but they are now being extended and improved.

The garden is a tilted bowl shape, divided in the lowest part by a spring-fed stream cascading gently through several natural ponds. Hostas, marsh plants and water lilies make a tranquil and relaxing scene.

Formal beds of mature trees and shrubs, heathers and conifers, are all cleverly built up and retained by natural stone and brick walls to take advantage of the sloping site. Two man-made vertical features complement the trees: sturdy rustic frames supporting climbing roses, an old wisteria, variegated ivy and honeysuckle.

Wellington Lodge was previously owned by a stonemason, and two intriguing gargoyles crouched under the bushes reputedly came from the Houses of Parliament.

Vegetables and fruit bushes have not been forgotten, but are so placed that specimen trees shield them from the house. A terrace and rockery make an excellent vantage point from which to view the garden, but paths invite you to explore.

Colehill
(Wimborne)

North Leigh House

B3073 from Wimborne centre towards Ringwood. Turn left into North Leigh Lane, and the house is about 3/4 mile on left.

Open for NGS and other charities. Teas. This is one garden where your dog is welcome – on a lead, please.

Built to a high standard in 1862 for Dame Ellen Glyn this handsomely proportioned Victorian house, now home to Mr and Mrs S. Walker, remains the focus in the wider beauty of the gardens.

The formal walled garden to the east of the house is prettily planted in pink, white and blue. There are hydrangeas at the summer opening, and a magnificent *Magnolia grandiflora* with its huge creamy-white flowers. The two arched pergolas provide shady retreats, and a brick and cobbled central roundel shows off an hibiscus to best advantage. This garden also includes a pretty tea room, and a greenhouse.

The pride and joy of North Leigh is the wonderful Victorian conservatory. Designed to match the twin gables of the south elevation with decorative barge boards in white, the pitched roof is supported on slim, fluted cast iron columns. The floor is of white marble slabs, and rainwater is brought inside in decorative leadwork. Several different abutilons adorn the house wall, and potted plants and ferns maintain the Victorian atmosphere.

Through a gate, a rhododendron lined drive curves round the west front of the house to sweeping lawns. The one nearest the house is attractive in May, when *Orchis Morio*, the green veined orchid, carpets the ground in what is believed to be the second largest colony in Dorset.

The lawns fall away in interesting terraces to the pond at the far end of the grounds. A badger sett and a new heather bed nearby provide an interesting combination; so far the badgers appear to be winning! The

The prettily walled garden at North Leigh House.

owners accept that gardening and wildlife are an uneasy pairing, enjoy the badgers, and replant the heathers. Deer, too, find the choicer shrubs, the best of which are reluctantly surrounded with protective mesh.

Through a screen of shrubs behind the pond, a small lake with an island of bullrushes can be found. Returning to the house you pass more mature trees and rhododendrons where the ground is thick with spring flowering bulbs. By the house a balustraded terrace and formal pond with fountain provide an excellent viewpoint for the garden, adding to its attraction as a successful combination of garden and parkland, on an enjoyably domestic scale.

Colehill

St Nicholas Close, 38 Highland Road

B3073 from Wimborne centre to Ringwood. Left at St John's Church into St John's Hill. Cross mini roundabout, then right into Highland Road (uneven surface). Park. St Nicholas Close is on right, down narrow drive.

Open for NGS.

Mr and Mrs A. Thorne moved to Colehill in 1970, since when they have built up a magnificent collection of azaleas and rhododendrons. More than 100 varieties of camellias are grown, most from cuttings in a mist propagator.

Of special note were hybrid rhododendron 'Sappho', white with a black/purple blotched centre; *R.* 'wardii', with loose pale yellow trusses; *R. macabeanum* with its huge felty leaves; *R. yakushimanum* with huge globular heads of pink buds opening to white flowers.

This is an acid gravel on clay soil, with mature oak trees adding an overlying cover of leaf mould each autumn. Besides providing ideal conditions for the larger shrubs, it also means that the sky blue meconopsis is easily grown, and the brilliant blue lithospermum which Mr Thorne has planted everywhere. Mrs Thorne has a small garden of alpines, in complete contrast to the size of the surrounding oaks and evergreens. There are shrub roses against the house and other plants to be enjoyed, but this is essentially a beautiful spring garden.

Corfe Castle

Rempstone Hall

B3351 Corfe Castle/
Studland. House is on left
heading east, after the
turning to Wytch Heath.

Opens for Red Cross and
other charities.

Rempstone Hall has been the Ryder family home for 200 years. The extensive grounds were laid out at a time when labour was cheap, and gardeners plentiful. Gradually the gardens became overgrown, and it is only recently that Mr and Mrs J. Ryder have begun to make the gardens more easily and economically managed, opening up vistas between the mature trees and wild rhododendrons that have taken over.

The house itself is very attractive, set well back from the road, with views of the Purbeck Hills around. The garden entrance is through an arch at the side of the house, with a millstone set beneath. There is a first glimpse of a small but colourful herbaceous border, with phlox, iris, day lilies, euphorbias, lysimachium and hardy geraniums. Beyond, the flower garden extends into parkland, with trees shadowing the wide grass walks below.

Rempstone is a garden that is slowly being reclaimed, and visitors will find future progress interesting. A large pond has already been cleared, and thinning of the rhododendrons has revealed a large rockery. Pieces of garden statuary have been discovered, and decorative lead water spouts that at one time must have gently poured water into the stone basins beneath. The rockery is now being replanted as the next stage of the restoration.

In between the wild rhododendrons are unexpected shrubs: a pretty white lace-cap hydrangea, and an ancient and enormous *Kalmia latifolia*. Everywhere there are carpets of ferns edging the stone paths that meander away in all directions, suggesting that there is still a lot more to be uncovered.

In the centre of the garden is a circular copper beech hedge, a quartered garden tucked away inside. There is a sheltered seat, with lavender, rosemary, potentillas and roses.

Closer to the house is a sunken courtyard with roses and herbaceous perennials in the nearby borders.

Cranborne

Boveridge Farm

Leave Cranborne on the Martin road (unclassified), and take the second turning right signposted Boveridge Farm. House is at the end of the lane on the right.

Open for NGS. Teas.

Beautifully framed view of open countryside, Boveridge Farm.

This garden was started from scratch in 1953, with an old rambler rose 'Félicité et Perpetue' being the only plant surviving from the previous tenant of Boveridge Farm. Mr D. Dampney has specialised in beautiful shrubs and trees, and the garden now is a delight.

There are three very distinct levels. The lower level has an herbaceous border, with foliage interest including *Acer pseudoplatanus* 'Brilliantissimum' and *Spiraea japonica* 'Goldflame'. Views across the countryside provide a lovely backdrop. Pink lily of the valley, Lenten roses and lime green *Euphorbia griffithii* add delicate colour under the shrubs.

The second level, in front of the farmhouse, has a formal pond with decorative fountain. Surrounding low stone walls are gradually being covered in varieties of ivy, and a gate leads away onto the lightly wooded hillside beyond, with a mown path inviting further discovery.

This is a north facing garden, but the farmhouse is well tucked into the steep hill behind. Even in spring the 'Banksian' rose was blooming happily under the eaves, and several clematis provided an additional riot of colour.

Because of the steepness of the land behind the swimming pool, rising to the highest third level of the garden, Mr Dampney decided mowing was too hazardous to keep the previously grassed banks. A large and very natural rockery was therefore constructed in 1986, with a gentle water cascade, and is the ideal spot for a large collection of ferns and wild plants.

The upper level of garden is the end of a clay cap, and therefore offers neutral soil rather than the alkaline conditions lower down. Camellias and rhododendrons thrive, together with magnolias. Lovely trees include a weeping *Prunus subhirtella* 'Pendula rubra', and the graceful Yoshino cherry.

Cranborne

Cranborne Manor

B3078 Wimborne Minster/Cranborne. The entrance to nursery and Manor is on left as you enter Cranborne.

Cranborne Manor gardens open Wed, 9 – 5 pm, April to September. Usually there is one Sat they are open for NGS. Wheelchair access. Garden centre open daily. Teas.

Cranborne Manor itself is not open to the public. The Manor was given to Queen Elizabeth I's Chief Minister, Robert Cecil, by James I, and is lived in by his descendant, Viscount Cranborne. The gardens were laid out by Mounten Jennings and John Tradescant in the 17th century.

Cranborne is synonymous with roses. There are hybrid teas in evidence in the garden centre, but it is mainly the old roses – Gallicas, Bourbons, Moss, China, Portland – that interest the visitor.

From the beech avenue approach mellow brick gatehouses lead into the south walled entrance court, where wide herbaceous borders over-

One of the two gatehouses at Cranborne Manor.

The Knot Garden at Cranborne Manor.

flow with colour. To the west of the Manor an Elizabethan Knot Garden is prettily planted and, beyond a smooth lawn, the unusual Mount Garden, rounded like a miniature hill. The Yew Allee provides a sheltered walk between high hedges to the orchard.

Beyond the orchard is the River Garden, where a channelled stretch of river divides the orchard from a border of primulas, hostas, and many other moisture lovers in between larger shrubs. Small bridges link the banks.

The north walled garden is particularly attractive. A stone balustraded terrace overlooks a grass walk between ancient espalier apple trees. A carpet of pinks beneath the trees smells delightfully old-fashioned. The borders in this walled garden are mainly white or very pale colours; roses, too, of course.

There are a Church Walk, Kitchen Garden, and a Pergola Walk. Climbers of every variety shade the paths. The return to the nursery is between high yew hedges, with small windows cut through on the south to give glimpses of the countryside and beautiful trees beyond. Green, Herb and Chalk Gardens, the latter sheltered by old chalk cob walls, are still to see. If the standard honeysuckles are in flower, they are a breathtaking conclusion to this lovely garden.

Edmondsham
(Cranborne)

Edmondsham House

B3078 Wimborne/
Cranborne. Turn right to
Edmondsham at cross-roads
just south of Cranborne.
House is between large
gateposts on left.

Open for NGS, also by
appointment (Mrs Julia
Smith) tel: Cranborne 207.
Wheelchair access. Plant
sales. Teas.

The grounds bordering the drive have been well stocked with mature trees, and in spring these shelter carpets of bulbs. The house is surrounded by lawns and gravel paths, with the vegetable garden and herbaceous borders in a walled garden to the east.

Vegetable gardening at Edmondsham is organic. Pests, which would normally be controlled by chemical sprays, are held at bay by planting marigolds along the rows. It is apparently effective, and certainly colourful.

The walled garden also contains fruit trees, a pumpkin bed, hazel bushes, strawberry beds and a partially sunken greenhouse which has been constructed from the old orchid house. The wide herbaceous borders are full of colour even late in the summer.

Edmondsham estate surrounds the house and gardens, the outlook in all directions being to open countryside. There is a small dairy behind the house which is open to visitors, and a beautiful stableblock with brick paved yard.

East Stoke

Stockford

A352 Dorchester/
Wareham, East Stoke is
approx 3 miles west of
Wareham. The driveway to
Stockford is on right, about
100 yards past the newly
named "Stokeford Inn" on
left.

Open for NGS. Wheelchair
access.

Stockford, the home of Mrs A. Radclyffe, is an old, thatched house with lovely latticed windows, set in 3 acres of woodland and walled gardens. The house has in the past been both a gamekeeper's cottage and a rectory, and is approached up a long drive through woodland. The house backs onto a garden which is walled on the north and east, giving lovely sunny borders.

Paeonies, iris and lavender combine with large cistus and shrub roses. The north wall shelters abutilons, honeysuckle, aconitum and rosemary.

By the house are mature cytisus: pale yellow, and gold and burgundy. Elaeagnus gives good early colour, next to the orange flowering *Berberis darwinii*.

Away from the house the gardens slope into woodland, with large rhododendrons, camellias and azaleas between the trees. Spring brings a carpet of primroses, while the strap-like leaves of colchicum, the autumn primrose, promise swathes of colour later in the season.

Ferndown

Conewood
308 New Road

A31 Wimborne/
Ringwood. Turn south
down Victoria Road to
Ferndown centre. At X
roads/traffic lights, straight
across to New Road. Past
Dormy Hotel on left.
Conewood on left, by 'bus
stop.

Open for NGS, also for
other charities and local
groups. Dates are usually
announced in the local
press, or tel: Ferndown
873646 for further
information. Plant sales.
Teas.

ABOVE *Conewood's Japanese
tea-house dominates one of
Dorset's more unusual
gardens.*

The front garden of this attractive house, with its small pond and neat planting of shrubs, gives no indication of the surprises to be found behind, where a Japanese tea house is reflected on the surface of a large pool. A red humped bridge arches across to the garden beyond, and Japanese style statuary accentuates the oriental scene.

The pool houses Japanese Koi – more than 100 of these large fish, in colours ranging from a pale champagne sparkle, through gold to deep orangey red and black. There is a tiny pumping house where the fish can be watched through an observation window in the side of the pond.

The Koi are Alfred Knight's hobby, and while they are undoubtedly part of the attraction at Conewood they must not be allowed to detract from Mrs Barbara Knight's garden. The area beyond the pond is hers, as far as the tall mature trees that mark the end of the plot. A keen flower arranger, she enjoys flowering shrubs: weigela, berberis, and wisteria are grown as standards to give room beneath for herbaceous material.

One of the most attractive features of this garden is that there are no hard boundary lines. Shrubs between this and neighbouring properties give an illusion of space, as do the trees at the bottom of the garden extending much further away than the true boundary. The plot therefore looks much larger than its one third acre, and the Japanese tea-house not at all incongruous in its setting.

This is a beautifully maintained and cleverly planted garden, and the Koi could make you spend far more time than intended at Conewood.

Fifehead Magdalen

The Old Rectory

B3092 Sturminster/ Gillingham. Turn left for Fifehead Magdalen, heading north. The Old Rectory is well beyond the church, on right.

Open for NGS. Plant sales. Teas available at Cox Hill, open same day.

The thatched house is surrounded by garden, which in turn opens out onto countryside – a lovely position. The front of the house is massed with plants in containers, with a rose bed to one side of the drive. Further tubs are ranged by the outbuildings with small shrubs and climbers, as well as fuchsias.

The large area of lawn is bordered by wide and irregularly shaped beds, fully planted with shrubs and perennials in a variety of colour groupings. Variegated foliage, gold and yellow mass together; pinks and reds; blues and silver. Mrs J. Lidsey's artist's eye for colour and form is very evident.

A rose arch frames a country view, and a tunnel of greenery shades the dry stream bed. A corner bed of various pink shades backs onto the mellow stone outhouse, with *Lavatera* 'Barnsley' making a good centrepiece, as in so many gardens this year. The annual mallows in pink and white fill in between the perennial plants.

Behind the house is a natural pond, bordered with hostas. A nearby bed of mixed colours makes a bright contrast with dahlias. Shrub roses make a good display early in the summer, and in August the tiny hardy cyclamen are beginning to carpet under the trees.

Gussage St Michael

The Old Rectory

A354 Blandford Forum/Salisbury. Turn south to Horton and Ringwood, then left at X roads. The Old Rectory is on right as you round a right hand bend just before the church.

Open for NGS as part of the Gussage St Michael village week-end, also the Old Schoolhouse garden. Plant stalls. Teas.

Another of Dorset's lovely old rectories, with a spacious 3 acre garden created by Mr and Mrs M. Grazebrook since 1977.

The house is approached along a drive, past shrub borders. The drive turns full circle, with a central gravel bed of alpines, topped by trailing pelargoniums and cotoneaster. The house is fronted by a lavender hedge, with climbing roses on the verandah. There is a new pergola at the rear, in an attractive paved courtyard.

Large lawns are gently terraced. Above the house they rise to a woodland walk and hedged wild garden, with *Rosa* 'Cornelia' making an eye-catching display.

The lower garden has large shrubs and mature trees, with a memorable collection of shrub roses. These roses are not for the smaller garden; they are at their best when allowed, as here, to spread and attain their full size. *Rosa* 'Crimson Bouquet' is very striking, surrounded by the softer colours of *R.* 'Baronne Prévost', *R.* 'Bourbon Queen', *R.* 'Ferdinand Pichard', *R.* 'Fisher-Holmes', and others. *R.* 'Garland' has completely taken over a large old apple tree – both blown flat by the storms but pulled upright by the local Fire Brigade and apparently none the worse for the disturbance.

Gussage St Michael

Old Schoolhouse

A354 Blandford
Forum/Salisbury. Turn
south to Horton and
Ringwood, then left at X
roads. Turn left at right
hand bend, and Old
Schoolhouse is on left.

See Old Rectory for details.

The perfect example of how to make best use of a difficult site. The lawns rise steeply beyond the house, with beds and borders sculpted into the contours and neatly edged around with brick.

Miss M. Wickham has incorporated some clever ideas. Three old trees in a line that had to be felled now form the base of a rustic seat which gives far-reaching views across farmland beyond. Another old tree has been reduced to a high stump, and smothered in honeysuckle.

A small paved area beside the house leads to the garage forecourt, with colourful tubs and hanging baskets. Pelargoniums surround an old well. Every available space is filled with colour. This is a delightful small garden.

Brick paving sets off the clever planting at the Old Schoolhouse.

Harmans Cross

Haycrafts Lane gardens

A 351 Wareham/ Swanage, turn right into Haycrafts Lane at Harmans Cross village shop. The gardens can also be reached, more unusually, by steam train on the Swanage Railway. The station at Harmans Cross is next to the village hall and its facilities.

Open for NGS, and other charities. Plant sales. Teas

These gardens open for the spring, and it was a cold day in late March when I visited. Dozens of people were taking advantage of this early opening of the season, which is preceded only by Kingston Lacy's Snowdrop Days.

Most of these gardens (eight in 1990) are on sloping sites, and good use has been made of local stone for walls and paths. Spring bulbs and colourful shrubs are on show, both in formal beds and more natural light woodland.

The few vegetable plots are well screened, and there is a delightful brick paved herb garden. Even the smallest garden makes use of – and manages to hide – a compost heap.

Early plants included *Clematis armandii* – evergreen with white sweetly scented flowers – which looks stunning next to an orange chaenomeles; also *Clematis macropetala* – deep blue 'Maidwell Hall', and rose pink 'Markhamii'. *Berberis julianae*, with yellow spring flowers, will colour well in autumn, and *Camellia japonica* 'Adolphe Audusson', deep red, and *Camellia x williamsii* 'Donation', silver pink, catch the eye.

Harmans Cross is one and a half miles from Corfe Castle, in the heart of the Isle of Purbeck. Views to the Purbeck Hills provide a lovely backdrop to these gardens, and a visit to Corfe Castle itself adds to the enjoyment of the day out.

Hazelbury Bryan

Broadlands

B3143 Piddle Valley road. Turn right at King's Stag to Hazelbury Bryan. Broadlands is ½ mile south west of Antelope public house, on road through Wonston, on left.

Open for NGS. See also local press (especially Blackmore Vale) for extra dates, or tel: 0258-817374 for an appointment. Parties by prior arrangement. Wheelchair access. Plant sales. Teas.

The present owners of this 2 acre garden, Mr and Mrs M. Smith, bought the property in 1975 when the land was open pasture. They have since hedged, planted, planned and achieved a garden of varied interest, with the added bonus of a small nursery.

The bungalow walls shelter climbers and shrubs, underplanted with a collection of hellebores ranging from the palest speckled pink to a deep inky purple. There is a paved patio area, and from there the garden leads away in a series of beds, paths and hidden borders.

A light woodland area has matured remarkably well in just 15 years, and is now being underplanted with hostas, euphorbias, bergenia, tellima, camellias and acers. A wide beech hedge separates this from the herbaceous border, itself backed by unusual trees and shrubs. The lower garden features a large natural pond bordered with variegated grasses and marsh plants. A dark green Korean fir leads the eye to the views over country to Bulbarrow. The pond is overlooked by a grassy slope now being given over to shrub roses, including 'Gertrude Jekyll', 'Emanuel', 'Charles Macintosh' and 'Marguerite Hilling'.

A second, more formal, pond is sheltered by sculptural beds of conifers and heathers. A 'cottage garden' has also been planted, through a honeysuckle arch.

Broadlands is very much an all-year garden, with plenty of foliage

The splendid garden at Broadlands enjoys distant country views.

plants to maintain interest. There are several magnolias, one of the most beautiful being pink *Magnolia x loebneri* 'Leonard Messel'. Scarlet *Anemone x fulgens* was in spring bloom, yellow *Paeonia mlokosewitschii*, and white *Exochorda x macrantha*. The lilac flowers of *Abutilon* 'Jermyns' had withstood severe frosts.

An early visit is not enough to do justice to this garden. The promise of the herbaceous border and roses will take you back. If you love your plants, most are labelled. Where a variety has occasionally slipped through the net, Mr and Mrs Smith are more than happy to share their knowledge.

Hilton

Hilton House

A354 Puddletown/ Blandford. Left at Milborne St Andrew, through Milton Abbas to Hilton.

Open for NGS. Wheelchair access. Plant sales. Teas.

Large entrance gates next door to the church lead up the drive to Hilton House, which overlooks a wide sweep of lawn, and is itself overlooked by the tree-covered hillsides of Bulbarrow. The garden has been mainly planted by Mr and Mrs S. Young since 1978.

The beauty of Hilton is roses. On the south side of the garden is a long flagged walk under arches and past borders, the scent of roses adding to the colourful displays on either side. Shelter is provided by a tile-topped wall, one border being edged by a dwarf wall, with poppies, phlox, paeonies and shrubs underplanted with dianthus. The wider bed separating the walk from the main lawn curves round to contain the lawn, leaving the walk to take you down steps and on to a small silver birch glade and orchard.

Hilton House, with wide sweeping lawns and a lovely rose walk.

A walled kitchen garden also boasts a colourful border of paeonies, and some beautiful mature trees — beech, oak — which also overhang the drive.

The gardens extend to the back of the house where trees and shrubs line a walk to the church. One tree is topped by a beautiful cascade of *Rosa* 'Wedding Day'.

Hinton St Mary

The Manor House

B3092 Sturminster/ Gillingham. Entrance to Manor House through large gateway, right hand side, on main road in Hinton St Mary.

Open for NGS, but other local events take place at various times, often advertising in the Blackmore Vale magazine. Wheelchair access. Plant sales. Teas.

Quite simply, one of the loveliest settings I have seen. The gardens are just a part of the attraction: the house itself, 17th century, in mellow Tisbury stone; ancient tithe barn; old stone walls; timbered lodge; all perched on a rise that gives magnificent views for miles over the Dorset countryside. Mr and Mrs A. Pitt-Rivers open the garden just one week-end a year, and it should not be missed.

A splendid avenue of beeches leads off the main road to the house gates, topped by herons. A pond and fountain with surrounding walls and hedges hide the south garden, with its lovely long rose walk stretching across the lawn.

Species and shrub roses tumble either side of a grass walk. A paved square filled with lavender breaks the progression, before the pleached lime alley.

Part way through the limes a right turn reveals an enormous fluted stone urn. Anything smaller would be lost in these large open spaces.

Pleached limes frame the sunken rose garden at Hinton St Mary.

Beyond the urn, decorative entrance gates open to a large walled garden behind the tithe barn, with old roses on every wall. The limes themselves are bordered by a low stone wall, and a hedge of the pink and white splashed *Rosa gallica* 'Versicolor' (Rosa Mundi).

Left of the lime walk, there is a magnificent sunken rose garden. Mellowed stone walls and steps enclose a very formal pond. The raised beds surrounding are filled with roses of every colour. The dark green of low yew hedges set this off to perfection and, on the skyline, narrow conifers frame the distant views.

Retracing steps to the house, a yellow and peach border is backed by shrubs and mature trees. Here one leaves the formal gardens to walk through parkland and enjoy the informality of the lightly wooded setting.

A garden, within a park, within beautiful Dorset; all can be enjoyed here. I saw it on a grey, cold day, and still came away enchanted.

49

Kimmeridge

Smedmore

Turn right off Wareham/
Swanage bypass,
signposted Kimmeridge.
From the west, turn right off
A352 Dorchester/
Wareham at Wool to East
Lulworth, and follow
Kimmeridge signs.

Both house and garden are
open every Weds from May
to September, plus Bank Hol
Mons. The house includes a
doll collection. Enquiries tel:
0929-480719. Wheelchair
access to garden. Plant
sales. Teas at Kimmeridge
PO, 1 mile.

Smedmore is a beautiful mellow stone house set just back from the coast
in a fold of the Purbeck hills. A glimpse of the sea can be had from the
main lawn south of the house, and the glorious gardens are a testament
to the skill of Major and Mrs J. Mansell who created them over 40 years.

Smedmore is a series of walled gardens, and the walls have been used
to excellent effect. The warm and sheltered positions provide early displays. A waterfall cascade of white wisteria vies with a beautiful double
lavender species for best effect, the lovely full red blooms of *Rosa* 'Étoile
d'Hollande' pushing their way up into the latter.

Winter sweet, campsis, and many clematis have space, and a vivid
honeysuckle *Lonicera x brownii* 'Dropmore Scarlet' – no perfume, but a
wonderful colour. The pineapple tree *Cytisus battandieri*, with its soft
grey foliage and yellow flower heads, has reached a mature size in the
warm south facing border.

One courtyard, the old paving stones as well as the walls throwing
back the heat, is a home for different herbs, overlooked by the acid
yellow flowers of *Fremontodendron californicum*.

Three small walled gardens are each a gem. Immaculately kept, they
used to be the coal and fuel yards for the main house. Now they make
beautiful use of the surrounding stonework, mellow brick arches and
gentle paths, massed with old-fashioned flowers.

The main south garden has herbaceous and shrub borders, leading to a
lightly wooded belt facing the sea. Several abutilons of different colours
provide intermediate height.

Notable shrubs and trees include yellow *Buddleia x weyeriana*; *Davidia
involucrata*; *Staphylea pinnata* and *Aralia elata* 'Variegata'.

Litton Cheney

The Old Rectory

A35 Dorchester/Bridport,
turn south signposted Long
Bredy and Litton Cheney.
Park in the centre of the
village, and follow the signs
through an old wooden
turnstile, up a steep path.
There is more level access
further back in the village.

Open for NGS. Plant sales.
Teas at Langebride House,
Long Bredy, open same
day.

The Old Rectory is the home of Mr and Mrs Hugh Lindsay, who have
worked hard to regain the 4.5 acre garden from the wilderness it had
become.

The house is perched high on a valley side, and most of the garden is
woodland, on a steeply sloping site that drops down in a series of paths
to the small lake and rivers running below. Nettles and ivy have been
beaten back, and now a carpet of comfrey has restored a very Victorian
look to the wood. A paved terrace on the side of the house is a wonderful vantage point from which to enjoy views to the south west in the
spring, before the trees are in full leaf.

A walk down through the woods is a must, but the paths are a bit
boggy at the bottom of the valley. Two palm trees were a surprise
among the very English foliage – this garden must share the warm air
streams that keep nearby Abbotsbury at 'sub- tropical' level. Purple
honesty and ferns add to the lush appearance of the woods, and a small
rose garden on the return should not be missed out.

There is a small walled garden behind the house, and a more formal lawn to the front overlooked by a thatched summerhouse. The Old Rectory itself is clothed in honeysuckle, a magnolia, clematis and roses.

Long Bredy

Langebride House

A35 Dorchester/Bridport road, turn south to Long Bredy and Litton Cheney.

Open for NGS and for other charities, also by appointment March/ end of July, tel: Long Bredy 257. Teas.

Langebride House lies in the bottom of the valley, surrounded by green hills and sheltered from the road by a beech hedge. The drive curves in around the wonderful 200 year old beech trees on the front lawn.

This is a steeply sloping site, and since 1966 Major and Mrs J. Greener have been implementing changes to make management easier. New walls have been built to enclose the vegetable garden, matching in style the old tile-topped boundary wall of the property.

Opposite the house, beds of roses and tulips flank stone steps leading to a formal garden enclosed in yew hedges. A pond, with old stone seats and statuary, is a peaceful spot to rest. Beyond the formal garden is an area of mixed woodland, providing a backdrop of differing greens to the

A woodland backdrop to the shrub garden at Langebride House.

more colourful foreground plantings.

Following hard frosts just 10 days before, the garden at Langebride seemed remarkably unaffected. A double white *Prunus* 'Ukon' was in full bloom, as was the mauve *Abutilon* 'Veronica Tennant'. They are in a walled garden, which does provide extra shelter, but were nevertheless much more advanced than many Dorset gardens at this time.

The herbaceous border is filled with phlox, hardy geraniums, iris and euphorbias. The wall behind is clothed in the deep pink *Clematis montana* 'Tetrarose', and nearby are the nodding blue bells of *C. alpina* 'Frances Rivis' and the evergreen *C. armandii*.

Yellow tree paeonies were in bloom, and pink *Magnolia x loebneri* 'Leonard Messel'. *Rosa* 'Boule de Neige', not yet in flower, completely encased several tree trunks – something to look forward to on another visit.

The formality of beech hedges, pleached limes and curved terraced enclosures contrasts well with the informal woodland backdrop, and the late spring open days promise much still to come.

Lytchett Matravers

Prospect House
113 Wareham Road

Unclassified road 1¼ mile south of Rose & Crown pub. House is on right heading south.

Open for NGS. Plant sales. Teas.

This pretty cottage faces onto the road, and is well covered with two varieties of wisteria.

The back garden has been most carefully planned, and makes excellent use of hard surfaces; gravel, brick, Portland stone and the local heathstone all provide the framework of paths, rockery and paving that are the bones of this well-structured garden.

The eye is drawn immediately to the elegant formal pond, designed by Mr Rowland Barnard, and built by him with Purbeck stone slabs cut by local craftsmen. The charming statue, marsh marigolds and spiky iris make lovely reflections, and the water also mirrors the Japanese-stye pergola behind. The pergola, also designed and built by Mr Barnard, could be adapted for use in any size of garden. It is rose covered, and makes an unusual change from rustic trellis. The eastern styling looks surprisingly at home in this most English of gardens, and should encourage many to be more adventurous with their garden design.

Through the pergola there are herbaceous borders of euphorbias, hardy geraniums, iris, paeonies and foxgloves. Fuchsias, too, are hardy between variegated weigela, shrub roses and rhododendrons.

Good use has been made of containers, placed at focal points with their cascades of geraniums. Feathery astilbes contrast well with the bold leaves of hostas. A mimosa tree casts its elegant shade, and the *Viburnum opulus* 'Sterile' by the rock garden was a mass of white snowballs.

The division of the informal grass/spring bulbs area from the formal close-cut lawn by an open paved path through which the grass has been allowed to grow is clever and works well. There are inviting seats.

Lytchett Minster

Bexington
Lime Kiln Road

Opposite school, at west end of village.

Open for NGS. Wheelchair access. Plant sales. Teas.

Bexington is two gardens in one: the mature, established garden behind the house, and a new garden adjacent that has only been added since 1988. A ditch between, running with shallow water in the spring, features primulas, hostas, and other moisure-loving plants.

A further link between old and new is provided by rockery and alpine beds surrounding a small pond, and a trellis that will eventually be covered with wisteria to echo that on the wall of the house.

Both sections of garden have herbaceous borders, with many of the more unusual plants. There are some beautiful roses: 'Julia's Rose', a light coffee colour, is especially eye-catching.

The new garden has a central heather bed, whilst the walls are gradually being hidden with tall shrubs and climbers. There are lots of penstemmons, a bed of azaleas, and a secluded green path leading through a fruit bed and shrub area.

Mr and Mrs Robin Crumpler have created a colourful haven in which it is very pleasant to sit and browse, and enjoy the clever blending of the old and the new.

Maiden Newton

Cruxton Manor
Frome Lane

A356 Dorchester/ Crewkerne. In centre of Maiden Newton, pass garage on left heading north west and look for green cottage on left. Frome Lane is a narrow turning by the cottage, signed to Cruxton.

Open for NGS. Plant sales. Teas.

The garden at this old manor house is still in its infancy, but each season sees a new border formed, a new idea implemented. It sits beside the River Frome to the south of Maiden Newton, at the head of a small valley which cuts away towards the sea. The views from the paved terrace at the rear of the house are of fields and farmland. The terrace is sunken, edged with stone walls and colourful borders. Stone urns of flowers and some elegant pieces of garden statuary make this a most pleasant spot to relax.

The house on the south is clothed with wisteria and clematis, and several climbing roses are making good growth. South west winds are kept at bay with hedges of beech and conifers. The main area of lawn has been formally bordered with herbaceous plants, with a massive phormium providing an architectural foreground feature. A trellis rose arch leads through to the further reaches of the garden, and is echoed by the arch at the side of the house.

Small walled gardens at the front are sheltered, with roses and borders of mixed colours. Mr and Mrs W. Hepher find time to tend a large vegetable and fruit plot, plus a small herb garden. In the garage yard roses, Morning Glory and clematis cover the walls.

This is not a well established garden, but it does offer the chance to see a garden maturing over the years. It is well laid out and colourful, with the lovely old house as a background.

Mapperton
(Beaminster)

Mapperton

A356 Dorchester/
Crewkerne. Turn left onto
B3163 to Beaminster.
Mapperton is signed on left.

The house is open to
groups by appointment, tel:
0308-862645. Gardens are
open from March to
October daily, except
Saturdays, 2 – 6 pm.

Mapperton is one of Dorset's finest manor houses, and the garden one of its best. The Tudor manor was built by Robert Morgan. Subsequent owners carried out extensive rebuilding, added a classical front to the north wing, and a Georgian staircase hall.

In the early part of the 20th century the estate was sold to Mrs Ethel Labouchere, who created an Italianate garden in memory of her husband. After Mrs Labouchere's death in 1955, Mapperton was bought by Victor Montagu, who added in particular the classical orangery, which now houses plumbago, vines and oleanders.

The garden is entered through the main gates, turning immediately left through an archway to the north walled garden. This part of the garden is mainly lawn, a gravelled path round the perimeter passing by wisteria, roses, pyracantha, magnolias, and clumps of Japanese anemones.

Looking east, the top of the orangery can be seen with a high wall beyond. The house is built on a plateau, and the gardens are deep in the valley below. The view is suddenly of clipped yew topiary, lily ponds, a wide pergola, and statuary. At the northern head of this valley is the orangery, with citrus fruit bushes outside enjoying the warmth in this south facing pocket.

A raised path hugs the walls, with a wide border of choisya, potentillas, phormium, climbing roses and clematis. There are several 'grottos'.

At the far end of the paved terracing – some of it dating back to the 17th century – a balustrade shields the drop down to the next level of the valley. Formal ponds are bordered by an 'upper walk' through a small shrubbery, with views across the valley to the house. Mature shrubs including camellias, and tall trees, lead to yet a lower level.

Mapperton's formal gardens fade gently into the Dorset countryside.

Here an informal grassy walk meanders through an arboretum of specimen trees and shrubs. The high west wall is topped by vast flower-filled terracotta urns.

Mapperton is a lovely combination of formal gardens bordered by natural countryside. Around the valley gardens the fields rise to the horizon, and the land stretches away to the south and the coast.

Marnhull

Cox Hill

Turn right at Marnhull PO into Sackmore Lane, right at T-junction, pass garage then Bat Alley on left, and Cox Hill is on the left.

Open for NGS. Plant sales. Teas.

Cox Hill is a pretty, faded pink and white house on the eastern slopes of the Blackmore Vale, with far-reaching views to Bulbarrow and the Dorset Gap.

The gravelled drive gives access to a croquet lawn, with a small and very pretty lily pond; yellow, purple and blue iris mingle with hostas. The silver foliage tree is *Elaeagnus angustifolia*, which has small cream/yellow flowers in early summer.

The main garden behind the house is a series of curved beds and interconnecting areas, with mature trees providing a light covering of shade. There are roses next to the conservatory, and a small paved patio.

A hedge arch leads to a paved garden overlooked by a summer house. Catmint mixes with golden thyme, lavender, erigerons and hardy geraniums. A small oval lawn contains a weeping silver pear tree on a carpet of gold *Lysimachia nummularia* 'Aurea'. From there it is just a step to the recently reclaimed orchard, and the herbaceous border.

There are no straight lines at Cox Hill — everything flows. Plants such as sisyrinchium, catmint, *Geranium renardii* and *Alchemilla mollis* have been allowed to spread and seed themselves freely, so colours carry on through the garden in a linking theme.

Captain and Mrs J. Prescott both have an interest in garden history, Mrs Prescott being a founder member of the Dorset Gardens Trust. Cox Hill was almost beyond restoration when they moved in. Thanks to their hard work, it is once again an attractive and entirely appropriate setting for this charming house.

Melbury Sampford

Melbury House

A37 Dorchester/Yeovil, Melbury is on left after turning to Evershot, heading north.

Open some Thursdays in June and July from 2 – 6 pm, for NGS and other charities. Wheelchair access. Plant sales. Teas.

The great Tudor mansion of the Strangways family is approached up a long drive, through parkland grazed by deer and famous for its trees. Melbury has undergone many changes over the centuries, and is now one of the largest houses in Dorset.

On the south side there is a broad paved terrace, with stone urns and lavender. The view is down a gently sloping lawn to the lake, with the land then rising again among trees to the deer park beyond.

To the west there are extensive walled gardens, where old brick walls provide shelter for herbaceous plants and climbing roses, and vegetables. The different styles and periods of architecture on the main house can be seen at close quarters.

Outside the walls of the more formal gardens, a gravelled path winds down to the shore of the lake, and along its banks. Melbury is parkland rather than garden. It is in a lovely position, and excellent for a gentle walk.

Melplash

Melplash Court

A3066 Bridport/
Beaminster, Melplash is on
left in village.

Open for NGS and other
charities. Plant sales. Teas.

ABOVE *Even vegetables and
herbs are decorative in
Melplash Court's very pretty
potager.*

An avenue of chestnut trees leads across parkland to Melplash Court – a
fine example of a small Jacobean manor house. The house is obscured by
trees almost until you reach a formal entrance court defined by rose and
periwinkle covered stone walls.

The garden is extensive, and on many levels. On the right of the drive
is a large pond, and a small running stream borders much of the land.
This has allowed the formation of a river garden edged with primulas
and other water loving plants, and the damp ground beyond is being
cultivated as a large bog garden.

Once it leaves the informality of the river garden the stream has been
channelled by edging with timber from the estate. Neat lawns sweep
down on one side, while a steep bank of shrubs and perennials ascends

on the other. There is a beautiful patch of pink and white astilbes. Small bridges and paths give access to the shrub banks, where massive gunnera leaves are tall enough to walk under. Everything is planted in large clumps and colourful swathes for maximum effect.

Further away from the house the water widens into a large lake, complete with island. There are already some fine mature trees, silver and burgundy foliage contrasting in the distance. The lake is to remain as natural as possible, yet still accessible.

A stable yard gives access to a small herb bed, and to a very pretty 'potager', its beds bordered with lavender. The croquet lawn next to the house complements a pastel shaded herbaceous border, and there are plenty of roses. A beech hedge provides shelter, and an umbrella yew is an eye-catching specimen.

Mr and Mrs T. Lewis have further plans for Melplash, and have already made many changes since they moved in. Tree planting continues, and also the making of a fernery along a shady fallen wall. This is a "don't miss" garden; most enjoyable.

Milton Abbas

Long Ash Cottage

A354 Dorchester/ Blandford, left at Milborne St Andrew, then left to Ansty. Long Ash is on right, next to the Rare Poultry, Pig and Plant Centre.

Open for NGS. Wheelchair access. Plant sales. Teas.

Tucked in behind a sheltering screen of trees, this cottage garden is a riot of foliage and flowers. A wide irregularly shaped border is packed full with phlox, day lilies, aquilegias, iris, cornflowers and scabious. Clematis are everywhere, climbing in the more usual fashion, but also rambling through ground cover plants such as cotoneaster: the blue single *Clematis* 'F. G. Young', beautiful blue double *C.* 'Vyvyan Pennell', light red *C.* 'Ville de Lyon', the deeper red *C.* 'Niobe', and *C.* 'Barbara Dibley' – to name just a few.

Mature trees provide a light covering of dappled shade, and give the garden a secretive appearance which goes well with its fully stocked cottage style. There is a caged vegetable area, and a very pretty rockery with small ponds. Sink gardens overflow with alpines.

OPPOSITE *Cottage garden colour at Long Ash Cottage.*

Minterne Magna

Minterne

A352 Dorchester/ Sherborne, about 8 miles north of Dorchester.

Open daily April to end October, 10 – 7 pm.

Minterne, the home of the Churchill family since the seventeenth century, was purchased by Admiral Robert Digby in 1768 and still belongs to the family.

The Admiral wrote in his diary that year: "Visited my new estate, valley very bare, trees not thriving, house ill contrived and ill situated." One wonders what persuaded him to part with his money! Perhaps it was the proximity of Minterne to Sherborne Castle, the home of the Admiral's brother the 7th Baron Digby, and whose grounds 'Capability' Brown was then landscaping. Although there is no evidence that he ever worked at Minterne, his ideas were surely incorporated into its improvements.

Shelter belts were planted along the tops of the hills, and park trees added to the bare hillsides. In the greensand valley below the house, a shrub garden was started. In 1785 a series of lakes and the Elinor bridge were constructed.

In 1880 the Hooker rhododendrons from the Himalayas began a collection for which Minterne is now famous. Seedlings from expeditions to China and Tibet were added in later years, and the rhododendrons have matured into one of the most lovely gardens. Many of the specie rhododendrons are still unnamed, and are identified by the name and date of the expedition only.

The woodland garden also has other splendid trees and shrubs. A canopy of beech trees gives shelter, the autumn leaf fall providing a deep mulch which is of enormous benefit to the smaller shrubs below. It seems entirely fitting that the original house, sadly riddled with dry rot and demolished in 1900, was used by Thomas Hardy as the model for Great Hintock House in *The Woodlanders*. The present house is one of the great Edwardian houses of England, built in 1903 of Ham Hill stone in a warm, apricot colour.

To the east, the lawns fall away to the lake at the bottom of the valley. The walk through woodland is in the shape of a large horseshoe, with a choice of paths at upper or lower levels on the eastern side near the streams and lakes. In spring and early summer the rhododendrons are at their best, but it is said that a rhododendron can be found in bloom on any day of the year. The festive December season is heralded by R. 'Christmas Cheer'.

The streams and pools are the best area for autumn colour, when Japanese maples and cercydiphyllums blaze with orange and red. In the summer there are hydrangeas, and a wild flower meadow. Seats invite you to rest and enjoy the tranquillity, shade and vistas that make Minterne so popular.

Minterne – one of the loveliest woodland walks.

Morecombelake

Pine Cottage

A35 Bridport/Lyme Regis.
50 yards past
Morecombelake PO,
travelling west, turn right
into Gibbs Lane. Pine
Cottage is first on right.
Parking is best in layby on
main road.

Open Thur and Sun mid
April to end May. Also by
appointment, tel: Chideock
89455 for details. Plant
sales.

When moving house the garden is not usually a major consideration; if it is not to your liking, you can soon replace or reorganise the plants and shrubs. When Charles and Barbara Lane decided to buy Pine Cottage, things were rather different. The vendor, Humphrey Welch, was an authority on dwarf conifers, and the garden contained more than 800. To change it would have been a massive task, and incurred the wrath of specialist growers and collectors everywhere.

Pine Cottage is set on the steep slope of St Gabriel's Valley with beautiful views towards the coast. Below the bungalow beds of conifers fill the slope with green, blue and gold foliage.

Dwarf conifers are not as 'easy care' as many gardeners hope. They need moving every 3 years or so as they grow; unless, of course, you are prepared to put up with large areas of bare earth and tiny trees until they become more established, or underplant with something 'sacrificial' that can be rooted out as the conifers gain size.

Behind Pine Cottage light woodland shelters a small collection of rhododendrons, camellias, acers and heathers; the main attraction, though, is conifers. This is a 'green' garden, minimal colour being provided by spring bulbs and herbaceous plants.

Pine Cottage is certainly a very different type of garden. It is well worth a visit though, and if you have the required acid soil at home you may find yourself at the beginning of a new project.

Mosterton

Oakmead

A3066 Beaminster/
Crewkerne, in centre of
Mosterton opposite PO. A
small lane turns off right,
heading north, and
Oakmead's entrance is just
inside on left.

Open for NGS. Wheelchair
access. Plant sales.

*Oakmead. The well designed
garden at Oakmead provides
interest in both colour and
form.*

A gravel drive curves in from the entrance gate, and immediately the visitor is faced with an herbaceous border, predominantly yellow and gold. This massing of one group of colours is evident elsewhere, and works extremely well. There is a large group of orange and yellow flowering shrubs and plants, with variegated foliage linking the different varieties. Marigolds, montbretia and potentillas are the main theme. A wide border nearer the house uses pale pink, blue and mauve.

Specimen trees have been carefully placed in the garden, with beds curved so that new areas are always awaiting discovery. Silver birch trees screen a new border of roses. A gravel bed, kept neat by an unobtrusive edging, shows smaller plants off well. The informality of the adjoining borders spilling over the edges is very attractive, linking the gravel bed into the main scheme.

In the main lawn is a large curved bed of heathers and dwarf conifers. The variety of colour, both in flower and foliage, makes an eye-catching display which lasts the year round. The front of the house is a mass of colour with hanging baskets, troughs and tubs. A formal pond on the raised terrace makes an ideal spot from which to admire the bold sweeps of colour produced by mass planting. Mr and Mrs P. Priest's garden should be high on anyone's visiting list.

Owermoigne

6 Hollands Mead Avenue

A352 Dorchester/
Wareham, turn north to
Owermoigne, then second
left. Right at T-junction, and
No 6 is on left.

Open for NGS. Plant sales.
Teas.

This garden in Owermoigne is packed full of interest. It appears much larger than it is, with open views across fields to the south west. The central feature is a small pond, with a gentle cascade of water. Surrounding small plants include *Saxifraga granulata* – the 'pretty maids all in a row' of nursery rhyme fame. There are plenty of alpines in between the paving and rockery stone. Mrs P. Baxter has a good collection of lewisias, and there are several sink gardens.

Herbaceous perennials come into their own later in the summer; surrounding shrubs include *Viburnum tomotosa* which was in spectacular flower earlier in the season. In the front, an imaginatively planted scree bed is a mass of colour. This is a most attractive and well-maintained small garden.

Plush

Little Platt

B3143 Piddle Valley road.
Turn right at
Piddletrenthide, travelling
north, up a steep hill signed
Plush and Mappowder.
Little Platt is the first house
on left as you enter Plush,
just before Brace of
Pheasants pub.

Open by appointment only,
tel: Piddletrenthide 320.

Sir Robert and Lady Williams open their garden at Plush by appointment, and it worth going to see the well-planned shrubbery that occupies the eastern half. Tall trees shelter the site to the north, and wide shrub beds have been planted beneath with grassy walks between. The variety of colour, shape and form makes it both interesting and attractive.

A collection of hellebores fill in under the trees. They are always good

Little Platt – Spring blossom for early beauty in the shrubbery.

value in a garden, their early flowers giving colour in the spring and the striking foliage providing clumps of different greens throughout the summer. The shrub garden is equally attractive early in the year, with spring flowering shrubs and bulbs.

The western half of the garden is a more conventional layout, with a large lawn, herbaceous border, and a colourful courtyard with small pond nearer the house. There is one large island bed of roses and a smaller bed for annuals.

Poole

Compton Acres, Canford Cliffs Road

The approach from any direction is well signed.

Open 1st April to end October daily, 10.30 – 6.30 pm. Tel: 0202 – 700778 for further details. A large free car park, small plant sales area, and toilets are available outside the gardens.

The classical elegance of Compton Acres.

Compton Acres, "reputedly the finest gardens in Europe", enjoys a beautiful site overlooking Poole Harbour and Brownsea Island. The gardens make use of one of the many chines, or valleys, that cut deeply towards the sea. They are small in area but cleverly designed so that visitors follow a winding path.

The suggested route visits gardens in varying styles, including the Roman Garden, Herbaceous Borders, Italian Garden, Woodland Walk, Heather Dell, Palm Court, Water Garden and Japanese Garden. The last of these is probably the most talked about, with pools, stepping stones, overhanging trees and Japanese statuary.

My own favourite is the formal Italian garden, a long narrow rectangle bordered by swathes of clematis, and rose beds in a variety of colours. The central pond has groups of delicate water-lilies, and reflects the tall enclosing trees at either end; shallow stone steps have balustrades covered with roses and topped with urns.

A cafeteria on the edge of the woodland has tables inside and out. An

inviting terrace overlooking Brownsea Island fronts the wine bar and creperie. There is also an ice cream kiosk and a small shop.

Where paths are steep or stepped there is usually a level and easier alternative, making the gardens accessible to wheelchairs.

Poole

Edgeways
4 Greenwood Avenue

Lilliput Road nr Compton Acres, travelling west. Turn right into Compton Avenue just past golf course, left into Fairway Road, left at T-junction. Please do not park on roundabout of cul-de- sac.

Open for NGS. Wheelchair access. Plant sales.

Edgeways invites you to walk through its planned vistas.

Clever planting in a one third acre setting has made Edgeways a 'must' in my gardening calendar. Mr and Mrs Gerald Andrews moved here in 1970 and apart from one or two mature trees have completely replanted the garden. The result is a garden of 'pictures'; clever foliage associations and contrasting shapes that carry the eye on in swathes of colour. This doesn't mean a regimented garden – it looks natural and informal – but it is very much a progression of spaces. It is a garden that asks to be walked through.

The pond is in a substantial hollow, the surrounding rockery beautifully placed. A small bog garden has also been formed at a lower level, creating conditions suitable for a wider range of plants.

Much use has been made of foliage, particularly gold, since this is an "all year round" garden: *Origanum vulgare* 'Aureum', *Lysimachia nummularia* 'Aurea', and a gold lamium are effective and striking ground cover. The grouping of a dark red acer, deep pink rhododendron, and sambucus with its limey leaves, works well.

The silky, silver-green leaves of *Convolvulus cneorum* are more attractive than the small white flower, as is the deep plum colour of *Heuchera* 'Palace Purple'. The latter groups well with *Artemisia* 'Silver Queen', *Cytisus battandieri* and the blue flowering catmint.

The white flowers of *Tiarella cordifolia* frothing above the pale green foliage live up to the more common name of Foamflower. This is a plant for which I shall find space in the border, together with *Astrantia major* 'Sunningdale Variegated'.

Foliage and shape are the mainstays of the garden, and although 1990 was the first year Edgeways was open to the public visitors will find a lot to admire and inspire.

Poole

52 Rossmore Road Parkstone

A348 Poole/Ringwood, south east into Rossmore Road. No 52 is on right.

Open for NGS. Plant sales. Teas.

Mr and Mrs W. Ninniss moved here as newly-weds more than half a century ago, and gradually exchanged parcels and pieces of land to form this one third acre plot. The garden has therefore grown piece by piece, and is now in the form of a series of 'rooms' which inter-connect along narrow paths.

The planting is full, a lush green profusion of shrubs providing the outline. One bed has golden foliage contrasting with a scarlet rhododendron, the whole edged with *Hedera helix* 'Buttercup'. This small ivy has light green leaves that turn rich yellow in the sun, and provides a most attractive edging while also smothering the weeds.

Azara microphylla is a useful small evergreen shrub, its deep yellow flowers having a vanilla scent. *Callicarpa bodinieri* bears tiny lilac flowers, followed by round violet fruits in the autumn. Autumn interest is provided by the foliage of such as *Cornus kousa chinensis* and *Euonymus alatus*, both of which have dark green leaves turning fiery red later in the year. Several acers also add to the display.

Syringa 'Bellicent' is a lilac not seen quite as often as other forms; the pink flowers are, I think, rather prettier. If you like a splash of white in a dark green border, try the single white rose-like flowers of *Rubus* 'Benenden'. This deciduous shrub also has attractive peeling bark.

There is a small pond guarded by a stone dolphin, with a gentle trickle of water around the pool plants including a beautiful variegated iris. Along the back of the house are more shrubs, and several roses. The Damask rose 'Madame Hardy' has a lovely scent, double white flowers, closely petalled, with a green eye. *R.* 'Cécile Brunner' is a China rose, with perfect small pink flowers.

The front garden is almost entirely taken up with an alpine scree, carpeted with saxifrage, daphne, dianthus, potentillas and geraniums amongst others. The gravel bed is essential for keeping the heads of the flowers dry, and keeps moisture in the soil for longer.

The remaining lawn around the scree is carpeted with hardy cyclamen, crocus and aconites early in the year. There is also a primrose bank, given as a present to Mrs Ninniss because her birthday coincides with their flowering.

Portesham

**Bridge House
13 Fry's Close**

B3157 Weymouth/
Bridport. Through
Portesham, Fry's Close is on
right travelling west just
past the village centre.

Open for NGS.

Mr and Mrs Geoffrey Northcote moved to Dorset from Oxfordshire. They left behind a Japanese garden which they had created and, to aid Mr Northcote's garden design service, felt they needed to create a similar showpiece at Bridge House.

Their choice of house was as much determined by the challenges set by the site as by the house itself. The plot was small, with a stream on the southern edge set in a deep ditch. This has been diverted to run through the centre of the garden, and is now the linking feature in this Japanese setting. It's stony bed breaks into a small waterfall at one point,

*Bridge House brings stylised
Japanese design to Portesham.*

and the darker pool near the bridge is a haven for trout.

In a Japanese garden there are traditional reasons why features are placed in a certain position. The aim is to achieve a feeling of tranquillity and calm, enhanced here by horizontal bridges spanning the stream.

A small pebbled island in the stream represents a mountain. It is reached by a bridge with a 'guardian stone', to prevent evil spirits passing by. A peninsula on the island is tipped by an Oki-gata lantern, on which all measurements have to be divisible by three.

Narrow paths in a variety of different surfaces link the changing levels of the garden, and enable you to enjoy at close quarters the many different plant varieties. I had expected something much larger, and was astonished at the interest that has been created in such a modest space. There are Japanese cherry trees – of course. *Prunus* 'Accolade' is early to flower, and is followed by *P.* 'Kiku-Shidare' and *P.* 'Shidare-Sakura'. *Prunus padus* makes a bolder statement on the far bank of the stream.

The Bridge House garden is exposed to sun, and to strong salt winds off the sea. This mainly low-growing Japanese garden has so far triumphed over the difficult conditions. It is an intriguing, and very different, style of gardening and makes a fascinating visit.

Portesham

Orchard House
1 Church Street

B3157 Weymouth/ Bridport. Orchard House is in centre of village, opposite the school and near the church.

Open every weekend all year, 11 – 5 pm. Open one weekend in year with other Portesham gardens for NGS. Wheelchair access. Plant sales.

This is a large garden, laid probably half and half to vegetables and flowers/shrubs. Mr and Mrs F. Mentern open their garden every weekend, and there are always plants for sale. These are raised from seed, and every penny earned goes to a good cause. Top of Mrs Mentern's list are Portesham church and school, and the Marie Stopes cancer fund. Other charities also benefit from the £1,500 that is raised in a good year.

The garden is packed full of plants, and there are several small ponds full of frogs which delight the local children. A small lawn at the back of the house is surrounded by paths and a paved area, with flower borders close by. The vegetables are kept to the edges of the garden, with greenhouses, cold frames and a shed where Mr Mentern restores old engines - also on display some Open Days.

There are wild areas at the side and front, where plants are left to seed and all kinds of unexpected foliage pops up. A small pergola and a raised terrace in front of the house provide shelter for some of the many plants and seedlings for sale.

Portesham

Possum House

B3157 Weymouth/
Bridport, in Portesham
village opposite the King's
Arms, left hand side,
heading west. A thatched
house on a bend in the road.

Mr and Mrs D. Yeates open
in conjunction with other
houses in Portesham as a
village event.

The main feature is a small natural lake, prettily overhung with trees, lying to the east of the main lawn. Herbaceous borders edge the other two sides, and I looked for plants which still looked good after the summer drought.

Artemisia schmidtiana is a very pretty prostrate perennial, with delicate ferny leaves in silver. It makes good ground cover, and every small breeze lifts the foliage and intensifies the silver. *Euphorbia myrsinites* also gives good ground cover, with blue-grey leaves along the trailing stems.

A raised alpine bed is a good example of how easy gardening can be when lifted a metre or so off the ground. At its best in spring, the alpine bed at Possum House stays attractive through the summer with interesting foliage shapes such as the sedums.

A fine old walnut tree shelters the main lawn, and the front of the house is becoming well screened with shrubs and fruit trees. The golden *Robinia pseudoacacia* 'Frisia' was planted about 1982, and is already a significant size. There is also a *Prunus serrula*, with bark peeling to reveal the polished red-brown colour beneath.

A small lake at Possum House is prettily overhung by trees.

Portesham

Portesham House

On the corner of B 3157 Weymouth/Bridport road and the village street into Portesham.

Open for NGS, together with other Portesham gardens.

Portesham House was the home of Admiral Sir Thomas Masterman Hardy. Black iron railings top a garden wall of Portland stone, with variegated ivy softening the outline. Apart from *Clematis armandii* by the front door, the house is solid and unadorned.

The side garden is more colourful, with shrubs and lilies in a wide south facing bed. A tree poppy, *Romneya coulteri*, with its white papery petals and yellow centre makes a splendid focal point. Behind the bed, a path runs by a rose covered wall.

The west lawn is dominated by a massive mulberry tree, its branches resting on the grass as well as reaching skywards. Believed to be about 300 years old, it suffered tremendous damage in autumn/spring 1989/90, and about one third of the tree was lost. Amazingly new growth is already covering the scars.

Mrs G. Romanes has planted a collection of Japanese paeonies in one bed. This is a lovely way to see them; much more effective than spreading them singly in an herbaceous border.

Behind the house, a paved area with a campanula covered well has shallow steps leading to the upper garden. Trees, shrub roses and a stream make an attractive foreground for the hills beyond. *Cornus kousa chinensis* is one unusual shrub worth noting, with its greeny-white flowers; also *Buddleia alternifolia*, a very pretty pink weeping tree much finer than the more usual forms, with pinky-mauve flowers.

Pulham

Cannings Court

B3143 Piddle Valley road. Turn east at X-roads in Pulham. Past church and Old Rectory on left, to end of lane.

Open for NGS and other charities. Wheelchair access. Plant sales. Teas.

Cannings Court is a working dairy farm, but Mr and Mrs J. Dennison still find time to tend the large garden, and are extending it year by year. The house is surrounded by paving overflowing with rock plants, and there are climbers everywhere. The old farm buildings are fascinating, whilst the main house has an extraordinary mix of 'cottage' front on the north and a Georgian style south front.

On the south, the house looks over lawns with herbaceous borders. This is not a clipped, well-marshalled garden, although it is obviously well maintained; plants have been allowed to twine and tumble, and the whole is a lavish collection of colour and form.

Beyond the lawn are the beginnings of a rose garden, with a rustic arbour. There are long grass areas where spring bulbs have been allowed to die down undisturbed, and old apple trees being slowly overtaken by climbing roses. A small pond is tucked in near the boundary hedge.

The garden is being slowly pushed out to the west of the house, and a new arboretum has been started. Mown paths link the young trees, and a new shrub border has been shaped round specimens that used to be dotted among the grass. The poppy border was awash with colour, as were the 'everlasting' flowers which are grown for winter colour in the house – hanging in big bunches, rather than in tight little arrangements.

The colourful display at Cannings Court extends over the walls of the house.

Pulham

The Old Rectory

B3143 Piddle Valley road.
Turn east at X-roads in
Pulham. The Old Rectory is
on left.

Open for NGS. Wheelchair
access. Plant sales. Teas.

When I started visiting Dorset gardens, I knew I had to be sub- con-
sciously looking for "my" garden. It proved very difficult to find — many
came close. The Old Rectory at Pulham, home of Rear Admiral Sir John
and Lady Garnier, was a total success. It has everything I enjoy in a
garden, in beautiful combination.

The long drive sweeps up to the gravel frontage of the house, a late
18th century building with 'romantic Gothick' front, now rendered in a
soft sand colour. White porticos and columns give it a classical elegance,
while the whim of a later architect added the castle-like crenellations
along the parapets. Climbing rose 'Albertine' scrambles by the door, and
clematis clad walls invite you in through the side gate.

To west and south the house is terraced in wide slabs of York stone.
The crevices, once neatly cemented, now provide a foothold for clumps
of soft grey *Dorycnium hirsutum*, pink and white daisies, lavender and
roses. The same York paving has been used as a wide edging to herbaceous beds.

Shallow stone steps lead up to a long vista of formal garden enclosed
by yew hedges. The borders contain herbaceous perennials, shrubs and
shrub roses. Muted colours have been chosen — no strident orange or

71

red – the picture enhanced by a decorative central urn. At the far end a beautifully shaped seat is enclosed by beds of lavender and catmint.

A yew arch leads off the formal garden to a large mounded rose bed topped by a Gothic style trellis for climbers. The south lawn ends in a ha-ha, with open countryside beyond. Two 'golden' triangular beds frame the view, across to Bulbarrow.

A large pond shelters under a clump of mature trees, the decorative fencing making it safe but also providing a most attractive enclosure. Yellow iris, waterlilies, and the giant rhubarb leaved *Rheum* are reflected in the water. Nearby shrub roses are underplanted with the blue hardy geraniums.

Ryme Intrinseca

Frankham Farm

A37, 3 miles south of Yeovil, turn by Q8 garage signposted 'Ryme Intrinseca'. Drive to Frankham Farm is about 500 yards on left.

Open for NGS and other charities. Wheelchair access. Plant sales. Teas.

Frankham Farm, a working farm owned by Mr and Mrs R. Earle, has over two acres of garden which have been developed from a flat field site since 1960. The drive approach is past raised borders of shrub roses, the edges spilling over with aubretia and other ground cover plants. Plants along the drive have been allowed to spread freely over the gravelled surfaces, disguising the edges between different materials.

There is a formal lawn and walled garden to the front of the farmhouse, with distant views over fields beyond. A wooden summer-house provides the ideal shelter to admire the wide mixed border of shrub roses and paeonies, with clematis such as 'Jackmanii Alba', 'Gypsy Queen', and the lovely double pink 'Proteus' on the wall behind.

The farm is exposed, and the gardens have been formed by establishing wind breaks of hedges and trees before attempting further plantings. Each section of the garden makes an 'enclosure' to give privacy within the larger site.

Near the house a pergola supports clematis and a vine, and also gives protection to a charming rock garden with anemones, fritillaries and trollius. Beyond this, the kitchen garden is neatly laid out and productive; the huge silver serrated leaves of the globe artichoke have also been used to good effect in the wild garden.

One of the latest sections to be planted is a lightly wooded area, underplanted with anemones. This is sheltered by a dense holly hedge, and *Metasequoia glyptostroboides* has a carpet of hardy cyclamen below.

Beyond the farm buildings, falling away to the south west, is a wild garden. Mature trees, hedges and shrubs have been planted in layers to filter the strong winds and give some protection. The mown paths weave through long grass full of euphorbias, bluebells, fritillaries and grape hyacinths. Evergreens provide foliage interest, and a charming naturalised patch of cowslips complete the picture.

Seaborough

The Old Rectory

B3165 from Crewkerne, heading south west. Turn left at second turning after derestriction sign. Turn right after approx 1/2 mile, to Seaborough, and in village take second left.

Open for NGS, also by appointment all year tel: Broadwindsor 68426.

The Old Rectory garden is large enough for massed plantings, and this has been used by Mr and Mrs C. Wright to great effect: *Alchemilla mollis* beneath roses, beds of euphorbias, hostas, dicentra and iris, providing a necessary theme in a garden that divides into several distinct areas.

A small front garden is entered through an arch prettily laced round with wisteria and clematis. A narrow path leads off to the main shrubbery/woodland. Mature trees including several magnolias give plenty of shade so ferns form an extensive collection, and there are also many lilies to give late colour.

The formal garden is behind the house. A paved terrace leads to a grass terrace. Stone balustraded steps edged with grey *Senecio* lead down to borders of tree paeonies, shrub roses and hostas. There is a small but charming stone owl on a plinth, bought in 1932 from a Swanage stonemason by Mr Wright who still has the receipt: "To one howle, 10/-".

Nectaroscordum siculum subsp. *bulgaricum* makes a striking clump – flower heads of pink/green bells supported on strong stems about 18 – 24" high.

Many Dorset houses seem to be blessed with sloping sites and beautiful views, and the Old Rectory is no exception. The terrace provides an ideal viewpoint.

Shaftesbury

14 Umbers Hill

B3091 from Shaftesbury, and at bottom of St John's Hill turn right at X-roads into Breach Lane, and bear right again to Umbers Hill.

Open all year by appointment tel: Shaftesbury 53312.

This is a small garden, sloping away from the bungalow at the rear to give magnificent views of 20 miles or more over the Dorset countryside. The garden includes a rockery, alpine sinks, patio plants, climbers, herbaceous, and colourful annual displays. It is particularly interesting to the clematis enthusiast, for Mrs K. Bellars grows nearly sixty different species.

The shrubs and trees have been cleverly planted to give contrasts in shape as well as colour. A Judas tree (*Cercis canadensis*) was in bloom, the first time in 7 years since it was planted, the pink flowers now being overtaken by the foliage. The pink *Indigofera dielsiana* has a lovely light covering of flowers – a dainty shrub for the smaller garden.

One corner is planted in stylised Japanese fashion. Stone paving, pebbles, a seat and sun dial provide the hard surfaces. Lines are softened by bright blue *Lithodora*, vivid yellow *Mimulus*, and spikes of blue iris. *Ophiopogon planiscapus* 'Nigrescans' is an 'evergreen' with black grass-like foliage. Lost against a conventional soil bed, it is very striking in pale stone.

Among the climbers are *Tropaeolum speciosum*, the autumn flowering nasturtium, and *Tropaeolum tuberosum*; but it is the clematis that win the day. Large-flowered varieties include *Clematis* 'Royal Velour', 'Hagley Hybrid','Ville de Lyon' and 'Niobe'. They are mixed with, and are climbing up through, roses; in Mrs Bellar's opinion, the perfect hosts.

C. montana 'Marjorie' completely covers a fence. The flowers are double, pink tinged green. 'Miss Bateman' is white with red/brown anthers; 'Horn of Plenty', a beautiful soft blue. There is also the herbaceous *C. heracleifolia* 'Mrs Brydon'. This is scented, autumn flowering, with large clusters of white flowers. The *C. viticella* hybrid 'Purpurea Plena Elegans' is another late flowering variety, with double red flowers like small rosettes.

A wigwam of tall garden canes provides support for seven or eight different clematis. If you copy this idea, make sure all are in the same pruning group. Clematis need regular watering as well as the correct pruning. Mrs Bellars also uses Phostrogen as a feed. The results speak for themselves.

Shaftesbury

Wagoner's Cottage

B3081 south east of
Shaftesbury, at bottom of
Zig Zag Hill. Cottage on
left heading out of
Shaftesbury.

Open by appointment June,
July and August only, tel:
0747-52877.

*An alpine bed effects a change
of level in the small garden at
Wagoner's Cottage.*

The front of this thoughtfully structured small garden is mainly laid to paving by the house, with a raised border backing onto the hedge and the road. Perennials and small shrubs have been naturally planted among larger rockery boulders. The front of the house supports climbing roses and clematis.

There is a pretty and clever linking of front and side gardens with a raised alpine bed, backed by potentillas and euphorbias. This bed widens out into another shrub border sheltered by conifers. Shrubs have been chosen for foliage interest – lime green euphorbia, variegated cornus, golden choisya and euonymus, and the scarlet and green photinia. Purple bugle has been used as effective ground cover.

A small vegetable and fruit plot has been edged with potentillas, clumps of day lilies, and creamy-white rose 'Nevada'. Even the narrow path around the back of the house is hung with large flowered clematis, and the garden shed is disguised with a pink climbing rose, deep purple clematis and white cistus – a lovely combination.

Shillingstone

Cobbles

A357 from Blandford
through Shillingstone.
Cobbles is on left in centre
of village, opposite Old Ox
Inn.

Open for NGS and other
charities. Plant sales. Teas in
village.

ABOVE *Delightful Cobbles,
linked by lovely gardens to its
hidden lake.*

The house has almost disappeared under wisteria, roses and other climb-ers. A delicate colour theme of pink and blue on the old cottage con-trasts with the border of hot pinks, reds and mauve that front the slate tiled pink washed extension. The main lawn is surrounded by scalloped beds of shrubs and herbaceous perennials – not a straight line to be seen.

It is a garden for exploring. A small winding path leads behind borders to a shady rose-hung pergola, and then either back to the flower garden or through to the neat vegetable garden. The latter is shaded by a spreading chestnut tree, and apples trained over an arched walk provide yet another path to follow.

Beyond the house mature oaks shelter a stream. With banks overhung with cotoneaster and spiked with iris, it borders a small silver birch glade and the fields beyond. The water has been walled here to make formal ponds, and then meanders on through little more than a grassy ditch prettily overhung by willows.

Giant hogweed rears its massive white heads, and Mr and Mrs A. Baker are making a bog garden. The grass slopes gently up past the stream, and breasting a rise at the top you discover a small lake complete with ducks. It is hard to realise that you are in the centre of a village, for you are surrounded by fields and open land.

An extensive collection of hardy geraniums fills the borders; they are, however, just a small part of this attractive and well-kept garden which is high on my visiting list.

Spetisbury

The Mill House

A350 south east from
Blandford through
Spetisbury. From this
direction, there is a school
on right as you enter the
village. The Mill House
drive entrance is directly
opposite, and is marked
confusingly by a County
sign which says "Footpath
to Keynston Mill".

Opens in aid of Dorchester
Parish, with local
advertising.

The Mill House is in one of the loveliest of settings — completely surrounded by water. On one side part of the River Stour flows past; the
mill stream sidles off in another direction; the mill pond, 30' deep, hugs
the house terrace. Within minutes of arriving I had seen a kingfisher.

The Reverend and Mrs J. Hamilton-Brown have lived here since 1975,
and began the garden with the usual clearing of brambles and over-
growth. The cultivated areas now merge gently into the landscape
through belts of wild balsam and a screen of willows.

The banks of the mill stream are steep, and have wide herbaceous

*An abundance of water makes
an appropriate setting, cleverly
exploited, at the Mill House.*

borders of yellow, gold and white. Day lilies edge down to the surface of the water, and the whole has become an 'easy care' area with the plants helping to keep the banks in place.

The terrace surrounding the house has probably the most unusual stone planters you will ever see – small coffins from St Peter's Church in Dorchester. A road widening scheme exposed the coffins behind the churchyard wall, and an offer to install them in the County Museum was rejected. They now brim with flowers – so much better than lying, forgotten, in a dusty corner.

Mrs Hamilton-Brown prefers to plant to a scheme, and there are some lovely combinations of colour in the garden: pink spiraea, lime green alchemilla, and poppies; blue leaved hostas and orange day lilies; more day lilies with white nicotiana and a blue spruce. Beds of tall grasses and bullrushes, and purple and plum coloured clary, retain a natural look.

A new bog garden has been started, for water is very much part of the garden. In spring it often covers much of the plot, washing away precious mulches and depositing a layer of mud over everything. See it in the summer, though, and you can't imagine how it is ever more than a beautiful backdrop to a lovely garden.

Stinsford

Kingston Maurward

Off the main roundabout at the east end of the Dorchester bypass.

The grounds are used for events throughout the summer, and make a most enjoyable visit. Watch the local press.

The formal gardens at Dorset's Agricultural College are like a spacious maze. Clipped yew hedges form rectangular and circular enclosures, with narrow gaps allowing enticing glimpses into other parts of the garden.

The lawns south of the house lead down to the River Frome where it widens into a large lake. Mature trees and distant views make this a lovely area of parkland. Closer to the house, on the west side, stone steps and balustrades lead to the gardens 'proper'.

There is a paved garden with formal pond, and further into the gardens a lily pond overlooked by a wisteria covered summer house. Between the two, a croquet lawn is contained by dry stone walls full of small plants. An upper walk here features penstemmons – I counted more than 50 varieties – and iris.

The beauty of Kingston Maurward gardens is that you can enjoy large collections. Most notable are the lilacs, and there are shrub roses, salvias, agapanthus, euphorbias and others. They give an excellent opportunity to compare one variety with another: everything is labelled.

In the centre of the yew 'maze' is a circular brick paved space with colourful beds of annuals. This leads into the wide herbaceous borders, backed by roses on tripods, with a wide gravel walk between. A second circular garden has an interesting stone trough in the centre.

The extent of old stone in steps and terracing, and the clipped yew hedges, make a formal contrast to the sweep of the lawn and lake below.

A classical framework of clipped yew surrounds Kingston Maurward's varied gardens.

Stratton

1 Manor Close, and Manor Orchard

A37 Dorchester/Yeovil. Branch left into Stratton village, Manor Close is on left.

Garden open days are printed in the Stratton parish magazine, and Dorchester library. This is usually June/July, and interested visitors should ring Mrs David (Dorchester 264593) near that time for up to date information.

These two gardens in Stratton are open once or twice a year for charity.

No 1 Manor Close, the home of Mr and Mrs W. Butcher, is a small, compact garden bursting at the seams with imaginative planting. Alpines are a favourite, and both front and back gardens boast a wide selection. The rear garden also has a most successful heather bed, backed by different varieties of clematis. Mr Butcher tries his hand at bonsai, and has a good collection of miniature trees and shrubs. There is a striking 'blue' bed, and a conservatory full of bright pelargoniums and streptocarpus.

Mr and Mrs G. David, at Manor Orchard, garden on a wider scale. They have just over 1 acre, bordered by the River Wrackle, with views to open countryside beyond. Clever colour combinations mean the large island beds of shrubs and herbaceous perennials are beautifully and imaginatively planted. The house is clothed with climbing roses and clematis, and there is a large pond.

There is plenty of space for vegetables and fruit, with apples trained over an arched walk through the garden. *Rosa* 'Seagull' is busy covering a new support – the old tree that used to be its host falling prey to the south west winds that whistle across the site.

Sturminster Newton

Ham Gate

Park in centre of Sturminster Newton, or opposite St Mary's Church. Walk through churchyard, or down Penny Street.

Open for NGS, together with the Old Schoolhouse. Wheelchair access. Teas.

Sweeping lawns down to the wide River Stour make a tranquil setting for Ham Gate. The house itself, mellow brick and dusky peach colour-wash, looks south to a superb horse chestnut that dominates this part of the garden. A small paved yard surrounded by colourful plants is an inviting sitting area.

The main gardens are to the east, where mature trees and shrubs punctuate the lawns. Changes are taking place, with the recent introduction of a large island bed. Hardy geraniums and shrub roses are being introduced, and a wider ranging scheme is planned.

It will be interesting to re-visit Ham Gate, the home of Mr and Mrs H. Barnes, and see how the garden develops.

Sturminster Newton

The Old Schoolhouse
Church Walk

Park in centre of Sturminster Newton, or opposite St Mary's Church. Walk through churchyard, or down Penny Street.

Open for NGS, together with Ham Gate. Plant sales.

Sir Charles and Lady Hardie have been most successful in the planting of this small, narrow garden. Enclosed by climber covered fences and sheltered by lovely old apple trees, each border is a harmonious blending of colour and form.

Immediate visual impact is achieved by a golden *Robinia pseudoacacia* 'Frisia' behind a purple sumach. The latter is underplanted with golden euonymus, and the border includes lime green *Alchemilla mollis*, *Spiraea japonica* 'Anthony Waterer', and yellow lupins.

Deep pink 'American Pillar' roses spread along one side, twined with a lighter pink and a purple clematis. Beneath them, a packed bed of choisya, escallonia, potentillas and roses is divided by a narrow paved path leading to the summerhouse.

'American Pillar' also covers a rustic trellis across the other half of the garden, framing a view of a lead urn on a pedestal and the white and silver border. *Philadelphus* 'Belle Etoile', *Cytisus x praecox* 'Alba', and the weeping silver pear, are all underplanted with smaller groups chosen to fit this delicate colour scheme.

Sturminster Newton

Rosecroft
Bath Road

B3092 Sturminster Newton, heading north. Rosecroft is on left of main road, opposite the Museum.

There is much to be enjoyed at Rosecroft. The garden immediately to front and back of the house is traditional – neat, lawned squares surrounded by borders of annuals, perennials, and rose bushes. Several old fruit trees shelter the back lawn, at whose end steps lead down through a small rockery to the vegetables.

This plot, on either side of the path, is a joy! Well ordered rows of produce, all weed free, and here and there a vivid line of dahlias or a patch of penstemmons brings colour among the greens. The asparagus beds were planted in 1930, and are still cropping heavily.

Go beyond the vegetables, through the hedge. To south, west and

Charming secluded village garden at the Old Schoolhouse.

Mr Dawes spreads the word locally when his conservatory is ready for visitors, which is usually late February/early March. Tel: 0258-72552 for an appointment.

north the countryside stretches away, while in the valley bottom the River Stour meanders between its banks and swans glide gracefully.

Mr H. Dawes is probably best known for the beautiful collection of nearly forty camellias that fills the conservatory in winter months, and local gardeners eagerly await the spring opening of Rosecroft for "Coffee and Camellias".

Tarrant Rushton

Charlton Cottage

B3082 Blandford/Wimborne, branch left to Tarrant Rushton at top of hill. Turn right at T-junction, first left to village. In village, turn right at T-junction and Charlton Cottage is on the left at end of lane.

Open for NGS. Wheelchair access. Plant sales. Teas in village hall when other Tarrant Rushton gardens are open.

This pretty old thatched cottage lies in one of Dorset's quietest villages, and is the home of the Hon. Penelope Piercy. The front garden is small, with several colourful cistus against the wall of the house. On the south side is a conservatory, filled in June with purple bougainvillea.

The garden behind the house slopes gently up to the fields behind, from where there is a magnificent view over the Tarrant valley. There are shrubs and roses planted in wide beds either side of the garden.

Shrub rose 'Madame Alfred Carriere' has climbed way up one of the old fruit trees, and R. 'Albéric Barbier' has a profusion of creamy flowers. The other half of the garden lies on the other side of the road, where there are splendid herbaceous borders, and a "chocolate-box" view back to the cottage.

One unusual plant that I had not seen before, and apparently accounts for most of the queries on garden open days, is dittany (*Dictamnus*). It has glossy dark green foliage, and purple heavily veined lipped flowers. It is an old cottage garden plant, and looks very well here.

81

The herbaceous borders frame Charlton Cottage.

Beyond the borders are the vegetables, including an asparagus bed, and a fruit cage. Light woodland leads down to the river. Mown paths lead between wild meadow, which encourages butterflies as well as a profusion of wild flowers. This patch used to be a withy bed, and several of the old willows still stand. New willows have been planted in replacement, the fine foliage allowing light through to the wild flowers and boggy area of iris. Part of this land floods in the spring, and so it stays a lovely natural belt between the cultivated cottage garden and the river.

Tarrant Rushton

River House

B3082 Blandford/
Wimborne, branch left to
Tarrant Rushton at top of
hill. Turn right at
T-junction, first left to
village. In village, turn left
at T-junction. River Cottage
is on left.

Open for NGS with other
Tarrant Rushton gardens.
Wheelchair access. Teas in
village hall.

The garden of River House can be reached through the garden of Tarrant Rushton House, and the two make an excellent joint visit. While at Tarrant Rushton House the river is subservient to the garden, here it winds its way through the grounds and the noise of the weir is ever-present.

Small footbridges criss-cross the water, the first leading over a boat-shaped island of hostas, ferns and primulas to the shrub walk beyond. The west walk passes several mature and spreading shrub roses, including the beautiful pink *R*. 'Ispahan'. I was surprised to find the roses

Aptly named River House, its gardens spanning the Tarrant.

growing so well in what must be semi- shade, a preference also shown by *R.* 'Complicata', which had climbed to a generous height up one of the old willow trees.

The fine silvery foliage of willows is set off by other roses, pinks and reds, with lavender and blue clematis climbing through them. This association of roses and clematis seems always to be successful.

There are bog plants: cream/pink/peach primulas, and the giant rhubarb. Bamboo grasses provide an effective screen at a bend in the river. A darker corner has been lightened with the cream variegations of euonymus and cornus, and the golden choisya.

Doctors A. and P. Swan have lived here since 1982. The pale terracotta thatched cottage is matched by the honeysuckle around the door, both blending with the gravel paths over which cotoneaster is making such excellent ground cover.

A landscaping 'bonus' is the tiny church, apparently tucked into a corner of the grounds. There is a church path leading to it, as River House was once the rectory. Whether it was ever called The Rectory I don't know, but River House is so much better. This is a garden planned around the river, and it works beautifully.

Tarrant Rushton

Tarrant Rushton House

B3082 Blandford/
Wimborne, branch left to
Tarrant Rushton at top of
hill. Turn right at
T-junction, first left to
village. In village, turn left
at T-junction. Tarrant
Rushton House is on left.

Open for NGS with other
Tarrant Rushton gardens.
Teas in village hall.

This house is approached by a long gravel drive, with a retaining wall on one side where the land drops away from the road towards the River Tarrant. Sheltered by this wall is a lower raised border with large clumps of hellebores, which have been described as 'a revelation' growing in this manner. The new growth finds its way up towards the sun, and the heavier old flower stems, still attractive as their bright lime green fades, hang down over the wall in a cascade.

The house is on a high terrace overlooking steeply sloping lawns, and mellow tile-topped brick walls divide the grounds. These walls provide shelter for wide borders, and there is a beautiful kitchen garden neatly box edged and divided by gravel paths. The border nearest the vegetables is full of delphiniums of every shade of blue, and multi-coloured aquilegias.

This is a large garden in which plants have to make an impact, and a foliage plant of note is *Rodgersia podophylla*. The large leaves are not unlike a horse-chestnut, and turn from bronze, to mid-green, then copper tinted as they age. Nearer the house are both white and purple forms of *Dictamnus* (dittany), an unusual old cottage garden flower.

Some of the plants have an interesting history: a *Crataegus* was grown from seed pocketed by Dr B. Blount when he was parachuted into the Greek mountains during the war; a 'clone' of *Tropaeolum tuberosum* was brought back by him from Peru in 1970, and now spreads happily through the garden.

Wareham

Culeaze

Leave Bere Regis on the Wool road, and after about 1.5 miles turn left, signposted Culeaze. The house is at the end of a long approach road.

Open for NGS. Wheelchair access. Plant sales. Teas available in Bere Regis.

The four and a half acres of Culeaze boast another of Dorset's sheltered, walled gardens, and this is a glorious mix — a gardener's delight. The garden is sub-divided by grass paths and a yew hedge, giving easy access and visibility to most sides of every bed.

The standard honeysuckle is a lovely sight in flower; the only others I have seen are at Cranborne. There are also several wisteria grown as free-standing trees. The twisted branches are interesting shapes in themselves, and are an unusual idea if no wall space is available.

Lieutenant Colonel and Mrs A. Barne fill herbaceous borders with wallflowers for an early display, with perennials taking their place. The purple flowers of honesty overhang paeony foliage, with the silver-splotched leaves of pulmonaria below. Shady beds hold Solomon's Seal, pink lily-of-the-valley, and a wide range of hostas. Shrub roses link with viburnums, and iris punctuate shady corners.

Culeaze has several very unusual plants. *Juniperus rigida*, a weeping tree with beautiful foliage, is so spiny that not even a clematis can be persuaded to use it as host. The tree originated in the Caucasus, as did the Alexandrine laurel which also thrives at Culeaze. This is the laurel that was twisted into many a victor's wreath in Roman times.

A splendid Judas tree occupies a corner of the main house garden, it's purple-pink flowers showered over the leafless branches.

On the south of the house is a small conservatory. It houses mimosa, beautiful when in bloom and lovely even just with the feathery grey-green foliage.

Wareham

Kesworth

A351 at Sandford, turn into Keysworth Drive almost opposite the school. At bottom of drive, "phone in" level crossing over railway to be negotiated, then onto estate.

Open for NGS. Teas in Wareham, but Kesworth is very suitable for picnics.

The house sits amidst 600 acres and is approached along a drive bordered with Japanese flowering cherries, beyond which are double rows of fastigiate oaks. These columnar trees have not been wholly successful, showing clearly how in places Kesworth is sheltered, and in others it catches the south-westerly winds.

The house is concealed until you enter between the red brick gate posts, topped with ancient stone vases. The ornamental vases are the first hint of Mr H. Clark's determination that Kesworth should reflect the best attributes of great landscape gardening - beauty, art and antiquity.

Facing the house clipped yew hedges enclose a lawn, creating a green outlook all-year. In the centre, a lead figure of a huntsman by Van Noste. Surrounding trees are full of blossom in May — probably Kesworth's loveliest month.

Behind the house a paved area provides a warm home for alpines around an ancient Venetian wellhead, and an old sun dial can be seen through a wrought iron gate. Brick pillars are topped by intricate baskets of fruit in Italian style.

A small shrubbery of azaleas and rhododendrons, a patch of old wal-

Kesworth's formal border, totally in keeping with the house.

nut and mulberry trees, and a line of kale pots brimming with geraniums add bright splashes of colour. A border deep with blue and gold iris maintains the formal atmosphere near the house.

The house at Kesworth was built in 1980, although Mr Clark has owned the land and been planning the estate since 1962. The result is in the style of 18th century parkland, with a formal area adjacent to the house.

On open days there is no restriction on where the public may wander. There are patches of typically English woodland, oaks with a haze of bluebells beneath and deer hidden deep within. A pond near the entrance is planted with English willows and is enjoyed by several species of duck. On a fine day the shore may be walked, with views to Poole and Brownsea Island. The marshland is a haven for birds. Galloway cattle with their calves complete the picture. Kesworth is a lovely place to visit.

Warmwell

Moigne Combe

B3390 through Crossways. Turn right by village hall, signed Moigne Combe. Drive entrance is on left.

Open for NGS.

Moigne Combe opens in the spring, with rhododendrons and azaleas providing garden colour in a natural landscape. There are views to the south across the valley to the Ridgeway beyond, a lake in the valley, and extensive woodland. The gardens fall away from the house terrace, with some intriguing old stone embrasures providing level sitting places.

A small 'heart' garden illustrates a totally different shape of bed, and Major General Bond has plans for the existing small pergola to become part of a woodland walk.

West Milton

West Milton Mill

A3066 Bridport/
Beaminster. Turn right to
West Milton, heading
north, and follow signs.
Very narrow lanes.

Open for various charities
throughout the summer,
advertised locally and in the
press.

West Milton Mill was the home of Kenneth Allsop, the writer and
broadcaster who wrote so descriptively about Dorset and about this
house in particular. Mr and Mrs P. Allsebrook have lived here since
1973.

The house is almost surrounded by water, the mill stream running
alongside and under the property. At the back, the house overlooks the
formal garden. A long rectangular lawn is edged by an herbaceous
border, with a magnificent lime tree overhanging white seats in the
distance. Hedges screen a swimming pool, and the more natural garden
beyond the visible boundaries. Lawns lead on to different views of the
mill stream, and a bridge across provides sufficient shadow for the trout
beneath.

West Moors

Highbury
Woodside Road

B3072 Bournemouth/
Verwood. Woodside Road
is on right, last road at
north end of West Moors.
Highbury on left.

Open for NGS on Sun
afternoons from April to
September, also Bank Hols.
Parties at other times by
appointment, tel: Ferndown
874372. Plant sales. Teas in
orchard, unless wet.

Botanists and horticulturists will be in their element, as this vast collection is clearly labelled. This is a 'green' garden; with more than 800 trees
and shrubs alone filling the half acre site.

Mr and Mrs Stanley Cherry don't plant for colour and effect. They try
and choose the right spot for everything they bring home, and it has to
fit in with its surroundings. They are, however, more interested in building up their extensive collections, and the variety is staggering.

There are a silver and variegated bed at the front of the house, an
experimental bed of conifers, herb borders, a layout planned for the
smaller garden combining planting and paving, an "ivy walk", and a
small orchard. The garden is very secluded, screened by mature trees.

Do look into the greenhouse. More unusual plants can be found there,
including the smallest known fuchsia, and the plant from which cor-
tisone is obtained. Not a garden for the 'hardy annual' enthusiast; but a
botanist's paradise.

West Moors

Moulin Huet
Heatherdown Road

A31 at West Moors. Turn
north into Pinehurst Road,
first right into Uplands
Road, third left into
Heatherdown.

Open for NGS, also by
appointment tel: Ferndown
875760. Parties welcome.
Plant sales.

The neat lawn at the front of this estate bungalow, with one central
prostrate conifer, gives no indication of the variety and expertise in
gardening that await behind.

Mr Harold Judd has been winning prizes at horticultural events since
1913. He has been 'Gardener of the Year' for *Garden News*, and has also
featured on BBC's 'Gardeners' World'.

The garden at Moulin Huet was started in 1970, when Mr Judd and his
late wife moved to a desolate patch of moorland, now West Moors,
bringing with them 3,000 seedlings and cuttings, all less than 12" high.
The garden is triangular in shape. There is no lawn. A series of paths and
trellises divide the plot into six separate areas, a 'secret' garden in which
it is only too easy to lose a sense of direction.

Mr Judd's love of alpines is evident in the wide collection of stone

Inside the greenhouse, Moulin Huet.

sinks immediately outside the back door, filled with colour. Not an inch of space is wasted. The greenhouse includes the pretty yellow Lewisia 'Harold Judd'.

In the main garden several shrubs, including a forsythia, have been 'standardised' to give more space for underplanting. A small water wheel feeds a miniature cascade, the splashes raining onto the nearby wall face which is home to the rare pale lilac coloured *Ramonda zerbica*. These alpines are seldom seen, and are too lovely to miss in this crowded collection.

Variegated lily-of-the-valley is an unusual addition to the garden, with its striking foliage; also *Poncirus trifoliata* (Japanese bitter orange). Espalier apples and vines are trained over a pergola, and lead to a wide collection of bonsai.

Wimborne

Dean's Court

The small road to Dean's Court is directly opposite the junction of High Street and B3073 in centre of Wimborne.

Opening dates in East Dorset District Council's garden leaflet, or from Wimborne Tourist Information Centre. Also open for NGS.

Dean's Court House was originally the Deanery to the Minster. The grounds extend to 13 acres, and include a lake, woodland area, a small but pretty herb garden, and a walled kitchen garden for organic vegetables.

The grounds include some fine trees. These include a Mexican Swamp Cypress, thought to be the largest in the country, and believed to have been brought from Virginia in the early 17th century. More recent plantings include several species of maple and horse-chestnut, Chilean Firebush, and a Japanese Pagoda tree.

Unfortunately in 1990 the gardens were hit by misfortune. Early storms felled many of the mature trees, and large areas are now being replanted. But do not be put off – the gardens are a most unexpected retreat in the centre of a busy town.

Wimborne

Kingston Lacy

B3082 Wimborne/
Blandford. National Trust
property well signed.

Wheelchair access. NT shop
open.

Kingston Lacy House is surrounded by splendid 18th century parkland with mature trees, many planted by Royal and other famous visitors. There are small areas of formal garden near the house, but they are not the main attraction of a visit to this lovely National Trust property.

In the spring Kingston Lacy has something special to offer. The local press gives dates of 'Snowdrop Days', the first garden opening of the county. The snowdrops carpet the raised beds of the Victorian fern garden, and also the lime walk. It is worth a special visit to enjoy this taste of gardens to come, and also to enjoy the Kingston Lacy estate at what is a quieter time of year.

Wimborne

Knoll Gardens
Stapehill Road

Take the Ferndown turning
(not the Ferndown bypass)
off the roundabout, east end
of Wimborne bypass .
Stapehill Road is on right,
Knoll Gardens well
signposted.

Open March – end
October, 10 – 6 pm.
Wheelchair access.
Cafeteria.

Knoll Gardens occupy a 6 acre site that used to be Wimborne Botanical Gardens. Kevin and Sally Martin took over in 1988, and began a programme of refurbishment and upgrading which has attracted the attention of television's 'Gardeners' World'. There are now more than 3,000 species of named plants in a compact and landscaped site offering something for everyone.

The gardening year at Knoll begins with a spectacular collection of azaleas, rhododendrons, camellias and spring bulbs. Mature eucalyptus trees spread their blue-grey foliage over the lawns, and there are many flowering cherries.

There is a well established conifer and heather bed, as well as extensive herbaceous borders. Most plants are labelled, and many are available from the adjoining plant sales display.

Rockeries, cascades and alpines occupy a large area at one end of the

Knoll Gardens – bog plants becoming established beneath the oaks.

site, with raised walks and seats to admire the view as well as the plants. Summer displays include fuchsias, and hundreds of colourful annuals. There is a wide Australian collection, a small but well planted bog garden, and a pretty woodland walk.

Wimborne

Priest's House Museum and Garden

In the centre of Wimborne, opposite the Minster.

Open Easter – end September, and a short Christmas season. Mon – Sat, 10.30 – 4.30 pm. Sun 2 – 4.30 pm. Wheelchair access. Teas.

From the back door a gravel path leads straight down a narrow garden to the mill-stream. The path is bordered by fruit trees, and there are several shady arbours with seats.

The garden has many unusual plants, including a Black Mulberry reputed to be several centuries old. The garden occupies one third of an acre, and includes a greenhouse with splendid vine. A rural gallery and working forge have been housed to one side, and at the bottom of the garden is a display of Roman tiles. In summer the garden is full of colourful annuals, the sheltered site seeming far removed from the noise of the busy town just outside its walls.

I found this an interesting small garden, much of its appeal being that it is in the heart of Wimborne and provides a very peaceful retreat. The garden has an 'olde worlde' charm that visitors will find hard to resist.

Priest's House garden, a quiet retreat in the centre of Wimborne.

Wimborne

Turnpike Cottage
8 Leigh Road

B3073 out of Wimborne centre, the cottage is on right about 100 yards from the junction with the A349.

The garden and studio are open from Easter until mid October, Sat and Sun 2 – 6 pm.

The home of Lys de Bray, botanical artist, promises something special by way of a garden, and the visitor is not disappointed. This small walled plot has been expertly planted to make maximum use of space, and overflows with plants ranging from the common to the rare.

A sunny courtyard guarded by a stone unicorn is overhung with climbers. Purple *Solanum crispum* faces the morning sun, it's golden centres echoing the climber *Fremontodendron californicum* which has decided to grow as a free-standing tree, and is making an excellent job of it. A

Luxuriant foliage and scalloped thatch at Turnpike Cottage.

collection of terracotta pots add their warm colour, with golden ivy and the purple hazy puffballs of allium behind. An old stone sink contains *Saxifraga x apiculata* and *Rhodohypoxis baurii*.

Paths of stone and brick, with pretty steps, lead under the mature trees to a pond. Everywhere the foliage is lush, with every shade of green from lime through emerald to deepest bottle; leaf shapes, too, are all here – sword edges, lacy ferns; upright, lax and twining. It is, as Lys de Bray points out, her library, and has not been planted solely to please the public but also to help her work.

There are conventional plants, as well as more than 30 different named varietes of ivy. More unusually, look for the phormiums, *Salix integra* 'Hakuro Nikishi' with its lovely variegated foliage, *Smilacena racemosa* with feathery white heads and glossy green leaves.

Turnpike Cottage itself provides one of the prettiest of backdrops. It is Victorian romanticism, with diamond paned cast iron windows, and a double scallop of thatch over the front porch. In Lys's workshop tucked away in a corner of the garden, you can see beautiful examples of her work. She is a Royal Horticultural Society gold medallist, and her botanical illustrations capture the charm of this walled garden and its many plants.

Dorset Soils

The different types of soil are the result of many factors, which can change from garden to garden. These include drainage, elevation, slope of the land (which can cause soil to wash down to lower levels), and climate. Since both elevation and aspect of the land are linked to geology, its influence on soil development becomes apparent. Specific inputs to the soil include mineral composition, the balance between acidity and alkalinity, and the particle size of the weathered rock.

Underlying the heathlands of the east are the Bagshot Beds. These acid soils cannot retain nutrients, and often have a white surface sand. They are naturally tolerated by conifers, birch, heath or rhododendrons. In contrast, the almost continuous ridge of Reading Beds running Wimborne/Bere Regis/Puddletown supports good mixed woodland. Normally acid, these soils can obviously support lime-hating plants like rhododendrons or azaleas, but also form good fertile loams for almost any gardening use.

The chalk soils are classically thin, alkaline, and low in organic content. While they support the glorious downland herbaceous flora, this may not be so much because of the soils' alkalinity as their shallowness. This cuts down 'competition' from over-shading shrubs.

The Greensand and Gault emerges from under the chalk, and forms the lower plateau at Shaftesbury and the 'caps' to west Dorset's cliffs. The Greensand often coincides with the 'spring line' and therefore has plenty of near surface water. Being naturally acid, these soils always show a dramatic vegetation contrast to the chalk above; for instance, supporting the azaleas and rhododendrons of Stourhead or Minterne, as well as deep rooted trees. The more sandy/clayey Gault is oak country (Okeford Fitzpaine) and is naturally very fertile. It forms some of the best soils in the county; but in the exposed flinty, gravelly sands of Golden Cap, Stonebarrow, or Pilsdon in the west, it is very different — the impoverished home for gorse, acid grasslands and heaths.

The Blackmore Vale is formed by the Kimmeridge and Oxford clays, a low lying area subject to winter flooding. Locally in the Vale the clay is covered thinly with sands, gravels or limey hill wash, which change its character dramatically. The Kimmeridge clay to the east is perhaps more undulating, and therefore better drained and more easily worked. These two clays are divided by the distinct ridge of the Corallian Beds. By its elevation this ridge is well drained, giving rise to good arable soils. These are favoured gardening soils.

There is a plateau of Cornbrash and Forest Marble around the

Caundles, Longburton and Stalbridge. Because of its 'brashy' nature these clayey areas also have good arable soils. If you can forget the stones, it is good gardening soil. The lower Fullers Earth soils are heavier.

From Burton Bradstock to Sherborne and into Somerset, the reddish brown soils are Inferior Oolite and Bridport Sands. These are shallow where covering the limestone capped plateaux, with few trees, yet are fertile because of both the lime and underlying rich materials. Rapidly draining, they provide light, deep garden soils.

The Lias in the west of the Marshwood Vale are heavy clays given traditionally to permanent pasture and oaks. To the east, undulating clays and sands give good, deep soils (Brown Earths).

There are the treeless limestone plateau soils of Purbeck and Portland, further exposed to maritime winds, and the Wealden clay vale from Swanage to Worbarrow Bay. Also the alluvial soils of the flood plains of the river valleys (Frome, Stour). These are potentially very fertile, but most are given to river meadows and summer leaze, because of flooding. The soils of the extensive terraces found about 20' above the flood plains are light, and tend to lack the body to give root support for heady garden perennials and shrubs. They are also likely to dry out quickly.

Geologically, Dorset shows the variety of rock types found across half England, with therefore a variety of soils to match. It is no wonder that garden character can change from village to village – and even from one end of a garden to the other.